THE
TWO-WHEELED
ATHLETE

Ed Burke

THE TWO-WHEELED ATHLETE

Physiology for the cyclist

Velo-news
Brattleboro, Vermont

Photo credits: cover photo of Mike Rosenhaus by Robert F. George; pp. 8, 43, 73, 85, 107, 115, Cor Vos; pp. 17, 35, 82, 112, Michael Chritton; p. 31, Steve Jennings; p. 59, Robert F. George; p. 63, Tom Moran.

First printing: March 1986, Second printing: November 1986.

Editor's note: The data in chapter 31 was prepared in cooperation with Mark Langerfeld and Donald Kirkendall and first appeared in the October 1980 issue of *Bicycling* magazine. Co-authors of chapter 10 are Tom Dickson, M.D. and Steve Fleck, Ph.D.

ISBN 0-941950-09-3

Library of Congress Catalog Card Number: 85-52407

Published by Velo-news Corporation
Box 1257, Brattleboro, VT 05301

Introduction

This book is a collection of articles which originally appeared in the pages of Velo-news, America's leading journal of bicycle racing. Because of the demand for reprints of those articles, and because much of the information does not exist in any other form, we decided to bring it together in this volume. The articles continue and update many of those in our first book on cycling physiology, *Inside the Cyclist,* and they also treat many new topics.

Though these 36 chapters do not cover all facets of exercise physiology and sportsmedicine, they represent some of the most cycling-specific information on these subjects available today. The detailed explanations and practical advice are sure to help both the newcomer to cycling and the experienced competitor. There is also much material to interest anyone who wants to learn more about the science of sport.

Author Ed Burke holds a Ph.D. in exercise physiology from Ohio State and is one of the very few specialists in cycling sportsmedicine in the U.S. He is director of new product development at Spenco Medical Corp., and was director of science, medicine and technology for the U.S. Cycling Federation and has managed U.S. cycling teams in the Pan Am Games, Olympics and world championships. A member of the American College of Sportsmedicine, Burke has written numerous articles for cycling and scientific publications. He is also the primary author of *Inside the Cyclist.*

—from the editors of Velo-news

Contents

Muscle tissue is composed of two basic types of fibers: fast-twitch and slow-twitch. A higher percent of fast-twitch can help kilometer riders such as East German Lothar Thoms, 1980 Olympic and multiple world champion.

1.
How muscle fibers affect performance

Lothar Thoms winds it out and rides another 1:05 kilometer to win a major championship. Nothing to it for a big, strong guy like that, right? Wrong.

Thoms must use almost every muscle in his body to ride at that speed. His muscles interact to push on the pedals, stabilize the upper body and create the forward thrust that makes him one of the best 1,000-meter time trialists in history.

Inside Thoms' body, muscles, bones and tendons collaborate like dancers in a well-rehearsed ballet. They create a motion that is smooth, effective and powerful. Of course, other riders in the kilometer rarely appreciate this artistry.

How did the East German reach this level of performance? Much has to do with government support, excellent coaching and sportsmedicine. But perhaps equally important is inheriting the right kind of muscle tissue.

The make-up of muscle tissue is like hair color, eye color and skin pigmentation in that we inherit it from our parents. Muscles can be different in fiber composition as well as size, and this difference can determine which sports an individual is best suited for. Scientists have shown that skeletal muscle tissue is composed of two basic types of fibers: fast-twitch (FT) and slow-twitch (ST).

Fast-twitch fibers are characterized by a quicker response to stimulation, a more rapid generation of force and greater peak force than slow-twitch fibers. Slow-twitch fibers, on the other hand, have greater endurance.

A person's FT/ST fiber percentage is easily determined by counting. A biopsy needle is inserted three to five centimeters into a muscle (the thigh muscle in a cyclist). A sample is withdrawn and examined with a microscope. The incision is closed with sterile tape.

Study of competitive cyclists

At the Human Performance Laboratory at Ball State University, my colleagues and I performed a study to determine if highly successful cyclists could be distinguished from less successful yet highly trained ones on the basis of selected muscle and aerobic characteristics. Could we find a budding Lothar Thoms?

Twenty-two male and seven female competitive cyclists (most of them road riders) served as subjects. The males were separated on the basis of success in national and/or international competition. Group A consisted of 11 cyclists who had won at this level. The remaining 11 males (Group B) had no outstanding race achievements to their credit. The females were riders of various abilities but were kept as one group because of the small number.

Muscle biopsies were taken as described above. Maximal oxygen consumption (Max VO_2) was determined so we would know each rider's aerobic capacity.

Physical characteristics of the cyclists are shown in Table 1. When compared to their counterparts in Group B, the elite A Group cyclists showed significantly higher Max VO_2. The aerobic data on the females is comparable to that found in other highly trained females tested on a bicycle ergometer.

While the mean Max VO_2 for the A group (67ml/kg/min) is not as high as reported for endurance runners, several factors may be involved. Max VO_2 determined while pedaling an ergometer is usually 5-8% lower than when running on a treadmill. Running uses more muscle mass and consequently more oxygen. In addition, most of our subjects were in the early stages of training.

A fiber composition of approximately 50% FT and 50% ST may be of benefit in cycling since most events require both endurance and speed. Sheila Young-Ochowicz, for example, posseses 47% ST and has been world champion in both sprint cycling and speedskating. (Of course, she was a skater first and even her shortest event, the 500 meters, is not a true sprint since it lasts 40-plus seconds).

In summary, the testing demonstrates that (1) the male and female cyclists show similar muscle fiber composition; (2) an extremely high percentage of either ST or FT fibers is not a requirement for success in road racing; (3) Max VO_2 is a good predictor of competitive success.

Remember, though, that most of the subjects were road riders. There may be "ideal" muscle fiber compositions for specific events. For example, a pure match sprinter or kilometer rider is a person endowed with a high percent of FT fibers. On the other hand, a muscle fiber composi-

TABLE 1

Mean (± S.E.) Characteristics of Trained Male and Female Cyclists and Untrained Men and Women

Subjects	Sex	Age (yr)	Ht (cm)	Wt (kg)	VO2 max (ml/kg. min)	Years Competition	% ST
Cyclist – A	M	24.6	180.0	72.8	67.1	5.6	56.8
		(3.5)	(1.0)	(1.4)	(1.8)	(2.0)	(4.4)
Cyclist – B	M	24.5	175.4	70.4	57.1	3.1	53.3
		(1.6)	(1.0)	(2.3)	(2.9)	(0.8)	(5.1)
Cyclists	F	20.1	165.0	55.0	50.2	4.2	50.5
		(3.1)	(1.8)	(2.1)	(2.9)	(1.3)	(5.4)

tion of 70-80% ST is ideal for endurance riding. A cyclist with this make-up would have the best chance of success in long-distance time trialing and stage racing.

While a significantly high percent of one fiber type can indicate athletic potential, data from a single muscle biopsy may be misleading or psychologically damaging to a cyclist. Scientists should not be in the business of predicting success. The biopsy is a research tool, not a destroyer of an athlete's dreams of success.

After all, there are several other factors that have a major bearing on athletic potential: strength, aerobic and anaerobic capacity, peak lactate concentrations in blood after maximal efforts, and years of training and experience.

While Lothar Thoms may have been given a head start toward kilometer success by his parents, having the right muscle tissue doesn't replace the need for hard work.

2.
Those puzzling endorphins

Recent articles in medical journals and sports magazines have presented the puzzling relationship between endorphin and exercise. In the early '70s scientists discovered that when a certain part of the brain was stimulated, test subjects had a sense of pain relief. Several years later, they found a compound in that brain tissue that had pain-relieving properties. Similar to morphine but even more effective against pain, it was given the name endorphin.

Evidence suggests that stress and exercise cause the release of endorphin. After any intense aerobic exercise, the body attempts to relieve pain by releasing endorphin into the system. It is said that endorphin is directly related to the "runner's high" and may cause addiction to exercise. Endorphin may also be the reason why endurance athletes say muscle tension is released after training. In fact, daily exercise may even lower the stress level of life in general.

The connection between exercise and endorphin is interesting, not only for what it may say about the mind-pacifying effect of cycling, but because endorphin has been linked to such varied functions as appetite, heat regulation and breakdown of body fat. It's no wonder, then, that these things are included in the physiological changes that take place with endurance training. Recent studies on the body's response to training have reinforced the link between endorphin and exercise.

In a study by Otto Appenzeller, M.D., Ph.D, at the University of New Mexico, there was a large increase in endorphin levels in 15 male runners after a 46-kilometer mountain race. These levels, which varied among the individuals, remained elevated for two hours following the event.

In another study, the blood plasma of long-distance runners was tested for endorphin before and after easy and hard running. The researchers discovered that the release of endorphin appeared to be related to the intensity of exercise. They also found that endorphin returned to the base-line level in as little as 30 minutes. These findings, along with those from New Mexico indicate that the type of exercise determines both the amount of endorphin put into the system and the length of time before it is used up.

Because endorphin decreases sensitivity to pain, some people think that it may cause athletes to ignore a minor injury until it becomes major. Some research has given weight to this theory, but as yet there is no firm evidence.

The release of endorphin might also explain the mood improvement following exercise, and the depression experienced by a regular exerciser who misses several workouts.

Researchers tell us that we all ride with an elevated endorphin level. This may be the very reason many of us continue to ride.

3.
Oxygen as ergogenic aid

The use of oxygen as an ergogenic aid in cycling is increasing. I have known riders who inhaled it before several stage starts in the high-altitude Coors Classic and others who experimented with it as an aid to recovery at the national track championships. It is well documented that the ability of the body to transport and use oxygen is one of the critical factors in endurance exercise. Increasing the oxygen content of the blood may improve cycling performance.

The oxygen content of inhaled air can be changed by increasing the concentration from the usual 21% to 100%, by compressing normal room air, or by doing both. These procedures might be expected to improve the transport of oxygen from the lungs to the blood and the transport of oxygen from the blood into the muscle.

Oxygen before event

Stimulated by the success of the 1932 Japanese Olympic swimmers, who breathed oxygen prior to competing, Karpovich began his study {2}. Subjects took two deep inhalations of oxygen before holding their breath and swimming for distance under water. In 11 out of 15 trials, the swimmers bettered their own records. In a second series of tests, Karpovich found that taking oxygen three to five minutes before a 100-yard freestyle swim had no effect.

In A study by Ebel {3} subjects breathed oxygen before, during and after a submaximal treadmill run. In the control study, room air was used throughout the test. The trials with oxygen resulted in lower pulse rates at rest and during the first few minutes of exercise.

Several studies {3,4} failed to find any benefit in using oxygen before exercise lasting more than two minutes. So it appears that breathing oxygen before competition has some effect, though it is limited. The time between oxygen breathing and the beginning of competition can be no longer than about two minutes, and the helpful effects will probably not last much longer than two minutes.

During competition

Numerous studies have shown that use of oxygen during exercise will increase performance. The activity can be performed with lower heart rates, lower ventilation rates and lower lactate levels. But there are few situations where oxygen can be used during actual competition, unless you want to replace a water bottle with an oxygen tank.

During recovery

After a hard kilometer or match sprint you will sometimes see the ambitious coach administering oxygen to his cyclist. Is there any evidence that this will aid the recovery process?

At present very few studies have been conducted on oxygen use after exercise. But according to the results now in, the benefit to later performance is small and probably inconsequential. Since in most cycling programs there is ample time for recovery between events, oxygen as an ergogenic aid may be of little use.

In conclusion, even if oxygen is administered before an event, the time between breathing it and the start of the race approaches the two-minute limit beyond which the oxygen can have no effect. The main benefit may be psychological.

4.
Tips for high-altitude training and racing

In the past several years more and more U.S. cyclists have been visiting Colorado for training and racing. Hundreds of riders stay at the U.S. Olympic Training Center for cycling camps during the winter. Summer brings many big races such as the 7-Eleven Grand Prix finals at the velodrome or the two-week Coors Classic.

Sea-level cyclists going to high country — such as mile-high Colorado Springs — should be aware of the possible effects of altitude on training and competition. Individual response to the conditions depends on a complex interaction of factors including health, training, type of event, degree of change in altitude, length of stay at altitude and one's own natural tolerance.

Not surprisingly, moderate altitudes (4,000 to 7,000 feet) present less of a problem than higher altitudes. The higher you go, the more cautious you must be. But remember that the change in altitude is more important than the absolute altitude. A cyclist who lives at an altitude of 4,000 feet won't have the trouble at 8,000 feet than a sea-level cyclist will.

You will find your stay at altitude more rewarding if you understand the environment and take intelligent protective steps against the conditions that come along with the clean air and sunshine: less oxygen pressure, usually low humidity, and intense solar radiation.

As you go from sea level to higher altitudes the percentage of oxygen in the air remains constant, but the amount of atmospheric pressure forcing the oxygen into the lungs is less. This reduced pressure of air at high altitudes makes breathing more difficult. Your body compensates for thinner air by increasing respiration and heart rate to maintain an adequate flow of oxygenated blood to the tissues.

How hard should one train at altitude? As long as we are talking about moderate altitude, there is no problem with training at normal intensity

Sea-level cyclists riding at altitudes of 4,000 feet or higher should take protective measures against the decreased air pressure, low humidity and greater solar radiation.

and the usual volume of sea-level work. Don't increase your miles or intensity just because the air is clean and cool, however. Keep in mind that recovery between repeated bouts of work might have to be extended a bit to maintain normal intensity.

Remember, too, that racing at altitude doesn't feel the same as racing at sea level, particularly for the relatively inexperienced. This was the biggest problem most lowlanders faced at the 1968 Olympics in Mexico City. Even those who were physiologically well acclimated to altitude were not adequately acclimated for altitude racing. One or two races at altitude is not enough to compete in a national or international event. Neither is it enough if you hope to beat veteran altitude cyclists.

Although a diminished oxygen supply to the blood is the most obvious environmental factor at high altitude, dehydration from low humidity

TABLE 1
Guidelines for Cyclists Visiting High Altitudes

	8000 Feet or Less		Above 8000 Feet	
Duration of Stay.	**For those whose normal training is:**		**For those whose normal training is:**	
	Steady Cycling	**Steady plus quality**	**Steady Cycling**	**Steady plus quality**
5 days or fewer	Normal training schedule at usual subjective intensity and for usual mileage or time	Same as steady cycling, but add one usual repetition workout adjusted for altitude	Comfortable cycling at easier than usual intensity for less than usual duration; no cycling would be OK	Same as steady cycling
More than 5 days	Normal mileage and subjective intensity. Add some tempo rides at slightly faster than steady riding pace every 3rd or 4th day	Same as steady cyclists. Include a normal interval session every 3rd or 4th day with adjustments for altitude	Gradually increase total mileage over two weeks. Use multiple rides to gain mileage more easily. When normal mileage is reached add some slightly faster rides for short periods of time	Same as for steady cyclists — include some short (less than one minute) rides at quicker pace with good recovery every 3rd or 4th day

is also a factor to consider. Since water is the basis for your body's oxygen transport system (blood plasma volume), loss of water dramatically magnifies the effects of the lower oxygen pressure in your lungs. Loss of 2-3% of normal body water creates a perceptible decline in performance. Dehydration is thus the main source of symptoms associated with altitude discomfort — headache, slight dizziness, mild nausea, difficulty sleeping — all of which usually happen in the first three days.

It is important to understand that alcohol, coffee and sugar drinks (soda) do not help. Each tends to dehydrate you more because alcohol and caffeine increase urine production, even though they momentarily decrease your thirst and fatigue. Moderation with alcohol is particularly important, since alcoholic beverages have roughly twice the effect at elevation than they do at sea level. Water and juices are the only effective hydrating agents.

A final note on food. A general carbohydrate diet, and a decrease in the amount of protein ingested, will lighten the load on your body as it works to restore a comfortable physiological balance.

Exposure to the sun at moderate to high altitude can have both acute and chronic adverse effects on the skin. This is especially true if you have very light skin. Redheads and blondes are particularly susceptible to skin damage. Sunlight is most intense between 10 a.m. and 2 p.m. when sun is directly overhead because fewer rays are screened out by the atmosphere. If you burn easily, avoid training or competing during this time of the day, or take other precautions. Clothes offer the most basic form of sun protection. A white jersey and hat will reflect the sun's rays. Dark colors are more likely to absorb the rays and retain the heat. Choose the material carefully. A loosely knit fabric will allow the rays to pass through; a tightly knit one will keep heat next to the body.

There are many different sunscreen lotions on the market, and most of them contain a chemical called PABA (para-amino-benzoic acid). This chemical blocks most burning rays but permits some tanning rays to get through. Pre-Sun, Sundown and Sungard are excellent sunscreens. You may have to apply these several times, depending on how much you perspire.

Gradually adapting to all the changes at a new altitude will help you perform your best in competition.

5.
The winning edge may be mental

Although many sports now rely on psychological training in their program, cycling has been slow to follow. Yet there is little doubt that elite cyclists succeed because of psychological as well as physiological capabilities. As riders reach the top levels of competition their mental training becomes more important. The cyclist who can best control psychological energy will probably have the decisive edge.

Mental techniques for improving performance are not new. It is interesting to note that the Soviets and East Germans have for years offered intensive psychological training to their athletes. Other countries are now following suit, and many have their own traveling team psychologist.

An area of major concern to many athletes is the management of stress, particularly before a big event. A technique developed by Dr. Richard Suinn of Colorado State University involves the use of relaxation and imagery to strengthen mental and motor skills. Dr. Suinn has worked with the U.S. alpine, cross-country and modern pentathlon team members. Dr. Andrew Jacobs is using this technique with our National and Olympic Team members as part of the USOC-USCF Elite Athlete Program. Many have improved their technique, concentration, memorization and aggression.

Relaxation stage

The technique begins with a 20-minute period of isometric-like tensing and relaxing of the muscle groups followed by the imagery session.

The first stage is as follows:

1. Find a quiet place to lie down. Close your eyes and think about becoming as relaxed as possible.

2. Make both hands into fists and become aware of how this tenseness feels.

3. Relax both hands and focus on the feeling of greater relaxation.

4. Repeat steps 2 and 3 with the following muscle groups:
— forehead: frown hard and relax.
— eyes: close tightly and relax with them still closed.
— facial muscles: clench jaws and relax.
— chest: take deep breath and hold until tension is felt, then exhale and relax.
— biceps: bend arms at elbow, contract muscles, then relax.
— thighs: contract and relax.
— lower legs, feet: point toes downward and relax.
5. Follow this with a deep breath and feel the total body beginning to unwind. Repeat step 2 to 4 two more times.

Imagery process

Immediately following the relaxation phase begin the imagery process:
1. Remaining quiet, take the first pleasant thought that comes and build upon it. Use it to become more relaxed and dwell upon it for 10-15 seconds.
2. Repeat this once or twice more.
3. Select an element of the event you are preparing for or wish to practice. It may be the initial burst of the kilometer, the pull at the front during a 100-kilometer time trial, whatever. Remain relaxed.
4. Switch on the scene (for example, just before the start command in the kilometer). Breathe deeply, retain the scene and continue to let the body relax.
5. Practice in your mind the skill you wish to execute to precision. Feel the motions as if everything were right on and this were a gold medal ride.
6. Make sure to complete the entire skill before you stop. Never practice a mistake.
7. Until your imagery technique develops, use short scenes. Then gradually lengthen them as long as you can remain calm and in charge of the process.

Through this technique you can reduce pre-race stress and actual improve your performance. The imagery technique can be used to perform under stress, in poor environmental conditions (bad roads, rain, gusting winds) and during recovery from injury. A cyclist who has been badly injured may hold back when he returns to the bike. The imagery technique can be used to eliminate this unintentional protective reaction while reinforcing skill.

The relaxation and imagery technique is only one example of how sports psychology is being used. The future promises new methods to help athletes achieve the maximum from their minds and bodies.

6.
Physiology facts for the female athlete

There is a new interest in sports physiology as it relates to the emergence of the female athlete. While women have competed successfully for many years, men have traditionally dominated the sports arena, especially in cycling.

How do women athletes compare to their male counterparts? By looking at the past records of the British Cycling Federation, Dyer {1} has shown that female cyclists perform at a lower level than males for all the road time trial distances (see table). Does this difference represent biological differences between sexes, or does it reflect social and cultural restrictions that have been placed on the female during her pre-adolescent and adolescent development? Data is very limited on female cyclists, but general comparisons between male and female athletes can be made.

Body build and composition

Body composition of the female athlete varies considerably with the sport in which she is participating, though the female athlete is typically fatter than her male counterpart. Most 18- to 22-year-old females will average between 22 and 26% body fat, while males of the same age will average between 12 and 16%. My associates and I have found that top female cyclists are in the 15% fat range while males are in the 8-9% range. In comparison to other female athletes {2}, women cyclists have lower values for relative fat than women in basketball (20.8%), gymnastics, (15.5%) and other varsity sports (20.6%).

Higher levels of the androgen hormones (testosterone) in the male are undoubtedly responsible for his possessing a lesser amount of fat weight than the female. Similarly, higher levels of estrogen hormones in the female are at least partially responsible for her greater fat weight. The mature female has a higher amount of essential fat, because of the fat in sex-specific tissue {3}.

TABLE 1
British road time trial records and the male-female performance differential (in hours, minutes and seconds, or miles covered)

1948			
Event	**Male**	**Female**	**% difference**
25 mile	58:35	1:05:40	10.82
30 mile	1:11:35	1:19:28	9.98
50 mile	1:59:14	2:16:53	12.92
100 mile	4:17:20	4:43:25	9.30
12-hour	251:87	220:53	12.43
1956			
25 mile	55:49	1:03:12	11.76
30 mile	1:07:30	1:17:44	12.86
50 mile	1:56:24	2:10:39	10.87
100 mile	3:58:28	4:34:03	13.07
12-hour	265:66	237:91	10.55
1976			
10 mile	20:27	21:25	4.53
25 mile	51:00	53:21	4.32
30 mile	1:02:27	1:12:20	13.26
50 mile	1:43:46	1:51:30	7.21
100 mile	3:46:22	3:52:16	2.58
12-hour	281:87	277:25	1.66
24-hour	507:00	427:86	15.58

Future research is needed to determine at what level fat becomes nonessential in female athletes. This question will soon be answered since more and more highly trained female athletes are developing and becoming available for testing.

Fat for fuel

A theory often raised is that since they have a higher percentage of fat and fat is an excellent source of fuel in endurance exercise, females should be able to metabolize it more efficiently and perform better in long distance events.

Recent work by Costill {4} discovered that matched male and female distance runners (same training mileage and Max VO_2) had the same ability to burn fat. What this means is that when males and females work at the same relative percentage of maximum capacity, they will burn the same amount of fats and carbohydrates.

This research demonstrated that those who suggest that women metabolize fat more efficiently because they have a higher percentage of it may have gotten their theory backwards. Females have more fat because they *cannot* burn it efficiently. In fact, women may be at a disadvantage in fat metabolism. Their cells release fat more grudgingly, since estrogen, the female hormone, blocks fat metabolism.

Temperature regulation

A recent television commercial shows a man and a woman on their bikes and states that men perspire more. If this perspiration theory were true, women would be at a disadvantage in long, hot road races. Once again, when males and females of equal training were compared, it was seen that both groups had the same sweating response. Actually, women have more sweat glands than men and with training they function more efficiently.

Strength

While women are weaker than men, this difference varies according to the area of the body. Their upper body strength is 43 to 63% less and lower body strength is 27% less {5}. The difference between upper and lower body strength is thought to be the result of usage.

Strength is extremely important in events requiring rapid acceleration, speed and handling of body weight. Thus, females are at a relative disadvantage in road sprinting and in track competition.

Both men and women can achieve large strength gains. Men show greater levels of strength increase and muscular hypertrophy (excessive growth). Women, on the other hand, can achieve strength gains of up to 30% and show little or no sign of muscular hypertrophy because of the lower levels of testosterone in their system.

Aerobic capacity

In comparing male and female athletes, there is considerable difference in Max VO_2 (maximum oxygen uptake) for most sports. The female is usually 15 to 30% lower than the male.

When compared to the values of other female athletes, six members of the women's national cycling team did quite well. Hermensen {6} reported a mean value of 3.65 liters/minute for six top Norwegian female orienteerers, which is comparable to the 3.58 l/min we found for our riders.

Research supports the thinking that women can be trained vigorously and can expect much improvement. The needs of the male and female athlete are essentially the same; therefore, there is no reason, on the basis of sex, to advocate different training or conditioning programs. Training procedures, however, must take into account the fact that women have smaller hearts, higher heart rates at rest and at exercise, smaller stroke volumes, less muscle mass and different response to sweating.

To a large degree the difference between males and females in aerobic capacity is attributed to hemoglobin concentration. When hemoglobin concentration is balanced, women appear to equal men.

Menstrual cycle

Since the menstrual cycle is an obvious physiological difference between the sexes, it is strange to note how infrequently it is included as an experimental variable in comparative studies of male and female athletes.

Findings are mixed on the effect that menses and the regularity of the menstrual cycle have on athletic performance. Some research has shown that the first menstruation occurs later in athletes, but no clear-cut generalization can be made. The regularity of the menstrual cycle has been reported to be sometimes unaffected, sometimes changed by athletic participation. When changes do occur, they seem to be found among women who participate in strenuous endurance sports, such as cycling.

The absence of menses and irregular periods usually to occur during the training and competitive season, but will disappear during the winter months. This variability could be related to the loss of body fat during the season (fat stores hormones) or to the stress of training (women in emotionally stressful situations sometimes experience menstrual irregularities). There seems to be no medical evidence that athletic training has any permanent adverse effect on the menstrual cycle.

Summary

The above effects and limitations cover only physiological differences between males and females. Other variables are the social, cultural and psychological factors which influence participation and performance. When males and females are competing together in certain events, limitations may need to be set in order to assure a competitive atmosphere. But by no means should women cyclists be stopped from racing against men.

7.
Exercise and the female cyclist

Cycling produces many changes in the body, some of which are anticipated and desired. But other physical changes may become a health concern for cyclists, who are unfamiliar with what "abnormalities" are normal in athletes.

While much has been written about the cardiovascular and physiological adaptations caused by exercise, little research has been done on other equally important medical changes that may occur. This is especially true in the area of how exercise affects female reproductive functioning.

Amenorrhea in athletes

Many recent medical surveys have revealed that female athletes have a higher degree of menstrual irregularities and secondary amenorrhea (cessation of menstrual periods) than the general population of women. Many people think exercise is the cause of this, but that is not necessarily the case.

As any athlete knows, when you begin training seriously, you may experience a change in sleep patterns and diet, a decrease of body fat, and possible physical and emotional stress.

When you try to coordinate social and professional responsibilities with cycling training you may find these activities also involve stress and confuse the picture. Exercise and emotional stress produce immediate and long-term changes in the body's hormone concentrations. Certain hormones are produced in response to stress, and they may in turn trigger the release of additional hormones. It can be extremely difficult to isolate any one of these variables to see its effects on menstrual irregularities.

Very few studies have investigated the life patterns of athletes before they became athletes. Many women who are amenorrheic or irregular before they become athletes, continue to be so after they commence training. This indicates that exercise alone does not cause menstrual problems.

Causes of amenorrhea

Every month hormones from the pituitary gland in the brain initiate the menstrual cycles. Two of these hormones, luteinizing hormone (LH) and follicle stimulating hormone (FSH), combine to mature an ovarian follicle, the casing that houses the egg in the ovary. Estrogen levels in the blood also increase at this time.

This huge estrogen level triggers an increase in LH secretion (called LH surge), which in turn triggers ovulation. During ovulation (around the 14th day of the cycle), the mature ovum ruptures the ovarian follicle, from which it then emerges, and migrates through the fallopian tubes into the uterus.

The remnant of the ovarian follicle begins to secrete estrogen and progesterone, which together prepare the lining of the uterus for implantation of a fertilized egg. If fertilization does not take place by the 22nd or 23rd day of the cycle, the uterine lining begins to atrophy. The estrogen and progesterone levels markedly decrease, the uterine lining sloughs off and vaginal bleeding follows, normally lasting from three to seven days.

It is well known that amenorrhea can occur in thin people or people who lose large amounts of body fat. It has also been shown that estrogen is metabolized differently in thin people or people who have recently lost weight. Some of the differences in metabolism may produce alterations in the way various glands function, particularly the pituitary and ovaries. These changes may result in menstrual disturbances.

Exercise too may have an effect on menstrual function. Hormones released by the brain (endorphins) may decrease the levels of hormones needed for normal menstrual function. Endorphins are released during exercise and this may be a possible link between these hormones and amenorrhea.

With no concrete evidence that exercise is the main cause of amenorrhea, a cyclist with menstrual problems should continue training but seek medical advice from a gynecologist who knows the importance of exercise. It should never be assumed that only training is causing the problems.

Menstrual cramps

Menstrual cramps are caused by the muscles of the uterus contracting, in response to a substance called prostaglandins (PG). A few days preceding menstruation, when progesterone levels suddenly drop off, the PG levels rise, triggering uterine contractions. The PGs also affect other smooth muscles in the pelvic cavity, and are thought to cause contractions of the intestine, stomach and certain blood vessels. This is a normal process, but unfortunately some women produce excessive levels of PG.

Clinical research has demonstrated that many women with dysmenor-rhea (painful menstruation) can be helped with new anti-inflammatory medications that help stop the production of cramp-producing prostaglan-dins. Along with the decreased PG in the pelvic cavity, there is less uter-ine contraction and the side effects of nausea, vomiting and headaches are dramatically reduced.

Many athletes have reported reduction in menstrual cramps after be-coming active in their sport. Research has not led to any firm conclu-sions as to why this happens. The release of endorphins may act as a natural pain killer and relieve the pain of cramping. Because of the na-ture of their efforts, athletes may also be able to tolerate more pain.

It should not be expected that a vigorous cycling program will provide total relief from menstrual cramps. In addition, just because you benefit by reduced pain while exercising does not mean that doubling the exer-cise will double the benefit.

Training and puberty

Many people believe that athletes experience puberty at a later age than their sedentary counterparts. They hypothesize that arduous training prior to menarche (first period) does not allow the endocrine (hormone) sys-tem to develop to a normal functioning pattern.

The fact that females who were very active as children also had delayed menarche does not establish cause and effect. It is conceivable, however, that delayed menarche will lead to greater athletic success. It has been shown that girls with early onset of puberty are usually shorter and fat-ter. Delayed menarche may produce a taller and leaner woman with bet-ter chance of success in sport. This is only a theory; the whole issue deserves further research.

Racing during pregnancy

To my knowledge no studies on humans have shown any harmful ef-fects of training during pregnancy. It is well known that physically fit women withstand the rigors of labor better than sedentary ones.

Cyclists should continue to train, with some modifications in their pro-grams. This will involve slowing down the pace because of the added work-load. Your training and exercise program should be discussed with your obstetrician for adaptation to your particular pregnancy. If any prob-lems arise (pain, bleeding, etc.) see your obstetrician immediately and follow his or her advice about what can be done safely and within your limits.

If you are pregnant, you should exercise in the cool part of the day.

Your body temperature should not exceed 101 degrees F., since heat has been implicated in certain birth defects. Take your temperature after exercise and if necessary wear lighter clothing or ride shorter distances. Prolonged heat exposure in pregnancy can lead to premature labor.

In my opinion, racing should be avoided because of the possibility of an accident and the increased metabolic effort and consequently increased body temperature associated with competition. You are concerned not only with your own safety, but that of the fetus.

Female cyclists should not assume that changes in reproductive functioning are due to vigorous exercise alone. Women should enjoy the benefits and pleasure of having a healthy and fit body and the joys and challenges of cycling competition.

8.
Myths about women

In cycling, there are many myths and superstitions. They are prevalent in the areas of nutrition, weight training, vitamins and fluid replacement. Another myth concerns female participation in longer road races. At the international level there is both conservatism and a lack of understanding in setting the maximum distances of the women's world championship road race and of stage races.

Based on research and available evidence, there appears to be no support for the different treatment of men's and women's cycling programs.

Research shows that females respond to endurance training in the same manner as males; therefore, restrictions should not be placed on women in endurance events. While it is generally true that women have less blood, a smaller heart per body mass, lower hemoglobin levels and a smaller cardiac output than men, training can increase the efficiency of oxygen transport. In highly trained females, when maximal oxygen transport is expressed in terms of lean body mass (total weight minus fat weight), the female is nearly identical to the male.

The problem lies in the fact that the female cyclist cannot leave her higher percentage of fat on the starting line; she must be carry it on the bike along with her muscle mass and supply it with oxygen. A study of lean female distance runners by Wilmore and Brown (1974) found that their maximal oxygen consumption was only 4.1% lower than a comparative group of male marathoners.

For many years women were kept from endurance events on the grounds that they could not tolerate heat stress over extended periods of time. Many of these misconceptions were fostered by poorly designed studies. Researchers used trained males and sedentary females and standardized work tasks that might be moderate for males, but significantly harder for females.

Once again, the fitness level of the female dictates how well she will adapt and respond to heat stress. A trained female cyclist will be able to elevate her cardiac output to a level sufficient to prevent a drop in

Research has shown that highly trained female athletes have nearly the same maximal oxygen consumption as their male counterparts. Is there any reason, then, to restrict the competition distances for such superb endurance athletes as 1985 world champion Jeannie Longo, front, and 1984 Olympic champion Connie Carpenter?

blood pressure and loss of blood flow to the working muscles when blood is redistributed to the skin in temperature regulation. Remember that acclimatization to environmental heat stress also adds to heat tolerance.

One of the great debates about female performance in athletics concerns menstruation. Should females avoid exercise and competition during various phases of the menstrual cycle? There appear to be differences among females with regard to exercise and competition during menstruation. Many have few or no menstrual difficulties under any condition, whether they are active or sedentary. On the other hand, a significant number of females have dysmenorrhea (disruption of cycle) or other menstrual difficulties that apparently are neither helped nor aggravated by vigorous activity.

Recently there have been reports of a total absence of menstruation in females who train for long distance running. This phenomenon may be related to low total body weight and reduced levels of body fat, since several studies have reported no menstruation (secondary amenorrhea) in chronically underweight females.

However, in a survey conducted before the '79 Red Zinger race, 33 female cyclists were questioned on the mileage ridden each week and the incidence of secondary amenorrhea. Approximately 12% of the women experienced this condition. These women were training between 200 and 300 miles per week.

Apparently, amenorrhea may be caused by many factors, but it is primarily characterized by loss of body weight. Cycling long distances may lead to decreased levels of certain hormones controlling various phases of the menstrual cycle and may lead directly or indirectly to amenorrhea. The role of cycling and the causes of these menstrual irregularities remains unknown.

On the subject of strength, it is well recognized that the average male is considerably stronger than the average female. Scores from several different studies suggest that men are approximately 30-40% stronger than women. However, when one isolates the lower extremities for males and females of comparable body weight and lean body weight, strength is similar, although the male maintains a distinct superiority in upper body strength. Strength training, formerly condemned as a mode of training for women because of its supposed masculinizing effects, is now recognized as valuable in building up the weakest element in the physiological profile of the female athlete.

While the male and female do differ in their response to vigorous exercise, there are probably more differences within the sex than between the sexes. The level of physical fitness makes more difference than gender does. Further, when differences are observed in trained males and females, in most cases the response is one of adapting and conditioning to chronic exercise. Because of these similarities, and because their needs are basically the same, there seems to be no physiological reason to keep women's road races so short.

9.
Cross anaerobic threshold to find endurance

Maximal oxygen consumption (Max VO_2) is one of the values found during an all-out test of cardiovascular fitness. Testing is done on a bicycle ergometer, normally beginning at a low level of work and increasing in regular increments until the cyclist can pedal no more.

Highly trained cyclists have levels betwen 70 and 80 milliliters/kilogram/minute. (Note that oxygen consumption, measured in liters/minute, is converted to milliliters and divided by body weight in kilograms to standardize the value for body size.) Lesser trained cyclists usually have values of 50 to 60ml/kg/min. Now the questions: Can Max VO_2 values tell us who can ride faster or longer than others? Can one definitely say that a cyclist with a Max VO_2 of 60 is more highly trained than one with 50ml/kg/min? These and similar questions must be approached with great care.

It would seem that a cyclist with a large Max VO_2 should be able to maintain a faster pace than one with a smaller Max VO_2. Why is it, then, that some national- and world-class cyclists {1, 4} do not have exceptionally high Max VO_2 values?

The answer lies at least in part with the anaerobic threshold concept. This term refers to the workload intensity during progressive steady-state riding at which lactic acid will begin to accumulate even during work that requires less than maximal oxygen uptake.

Importance to time trialists

A person's anaerobic threshold is a critical factor in determining potential to perform prolonged physical exercise. In cycling, individual and

Having a high anaerobic threshold is especially important to the time trialist, who must be able to sustain a high level of performance without the chance for recovery that mass-start racing provides.

team time trials both require a high anaerobic threshold, which may or may not relate to a high Max VO_2. Suppose that three cyclists (1, 2 and 3) have respective Max VO_2s of 75, 70 and 70ml/kg/min. Cyclists 1 and 3 have high anaerobic thresholds of 60 and 55ml/kg/min. while cyclist 2 has been laying off the training and has an anaerobic threshold of only 45. In a long distance race, cyclist 1 can maintain a pace requiring 60ml/kg/min and build up very little lactic acid, whereas cyclists 2 and 3, in order to keep up, must work anaerobically and therefore produce more lactic acid.

How do you know when your anaerobic threshold has been reached? When you begin riding, ventilation increases rapidly and then climbs linearly with the increase in oxygen consumption (VO_2). As the effort goes from moderate to intense, you reach a point where ventilation increases more rapidly than VO_2.

The graph

The graph shows the ventilatory response of two cyclists to a Max VO_2 test on a bicycle ergometer. Cyclist A has a lower Max VO_2 and anaerobic threshold than cyclist B. It can be seen that the breakaway point of

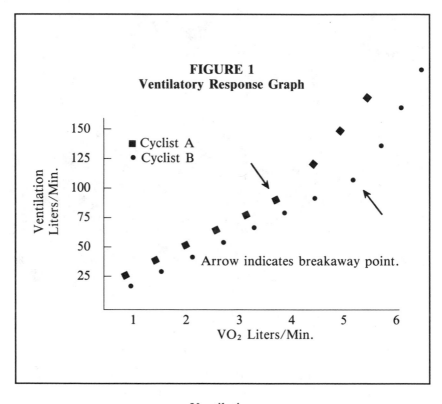

FIGURE 1
Ventilatory Response Graph

Arrow indicates breakaway point.

Ventilation
Liters/Min.

ventilation is at a higher absolute and relative workload in cyclist B. For example, at a workload requiring 4.5 liter/min of oxygen, cyclist A's ventilation would be approximately 25 liter/min higher than cyclist B's. This extra work simply to breathe would eventually take its toll on cyclist A.

This breakaway point of ventilation is a result of the buffering action of lactic acid in the blood. Excess carbon dioxide is generated from the reaction of sodium bicarbonate and the lactic acid that is beginning to accumulate. You are beginning to hyperventilate in order to blow off the excess CO_2.

The cyclist with a lower anaerobic threshold is also at a disadvantage when it comes to using fats as an energy source. Lactic acid in the blood has been shown to interfere with the mobilization of fatty acid {2,3}. The effective use of fat plays an important role in endurance exercise since fats release 9.45 kilocalories of energy per gram while carbohydrates release only 4.1 kilocalories. Fat stores equal 50,000-70,000 kilocalories in an athlete compared to carbohydrate stores of 2,000 kilocalories.

In a road race, the highly trained cyclist who operates at 80-85% of his Max VO_2 while accumulating very little lactic acid can obtain a relatively great amount of energy from fat stores. On the other hand, a less well-conditioned rider can complete the first 75% of the race with some ease, but then experience the "bonk" in the final miles. Remember, when glycogen stores are depleted, muscular effort becomes nearly impossible.

Improving anaerobic threshold

What form of training can best improve anaerobic threshold? Most of the current research has focused on the "duration" of the training load and the "intensity."

Before using endurance training to increase anaerobic threshold you need to know your best time for a 25-mile time trial on a level course. (If, for example, you recorded 60 minutes, then your pace is 2:24 per mile.) On days you designate for anaerobic threshold training, ride your miles at approximately 10-15 second per mile faster than your TT pace. Initially do 10 miles and work your way up to 15. Don't be in a hurry to up the mileage — give your body a chance to adapt to the stress. When you reach 15 miles, then quicken the pace another 10-15 seconds and go back to 10 miles, eventually working up to 15 again.

If you are more inclined to interval training or are limited by time, try this: perform work intervals of two to three minutes at intensities equivalent to 90-100% of Max VO_2, spaced with equal intervals of moderate pedaling. Begin with a comfortable amount and increase as the season progresses.

Success as an endurance cyclist is related to your anaerobic threshold. You can increase your with hard-paced endurance training and interval training.

10.
Lactic acid testing yields tips for training

During moderate levels of cycling, a rider's energy demands are adequately met by the aerobic breakdown of carbohydrates and fats. In biochemical terms, a sufficient amount of ATP (the energy source for muscular work) is made available, and a person is able to ride for several hours.

Competitive track cycling, on the other hand, requires intense activity from a large muscle mass and accelerated breathing. This favors involvement of anaerobic energy release and a production of lactic acid that far exceeds the body's ability to break it down. The result is a build up of lactic acid in the blood, which acidifies the environment of the muscle until it can no longer contract.

The feeling is familiar to many of us: muscle pain, cramping and weakness. Following the anaerobic activity, breathing remains rapid as the muscles and liver break down the tremendous buildup of lactic acid. Once this is accomplished, normal breathing rhythm returns and another hard effort can be made.

Testing for lactate
During the summer of 1980, we had the opportunity to investigate the blood lactic acid (lactate) concentrations of well-trained track cyclists during competition at the national championships in San Diego. The study included 19 males competing in various events. Thirteen of the cyclists were present or past members of Olympic, Pan-American, world or national teams. We investigated how much lactate was produced so we could advise them how to train in ways that reduce it or make it more tolerable.

This study could not have been accomplished without the support and use of the U.S. Olympic Committee's Sports Medicine Mobile Laboratory. A blood sample was taken from an arm vein five minutes after the cyclist completed his event. This five-minute interval allowed lactic acid to diffuse from the muscles to the blood and reach maximum. Samples were also obtained from four cyclists at rest to use for comparison.

Six samples were drawn after the one-kilometer time trial (mean time 70.86 seconds), and seven after the match sprints (mean time approximately 11 seconds). One cyclist was tested twice in the match sprints. After the team pursuit (mean time 288 seconds), five samples were drawn.

Likewise, 12 samples were drawn during various rounds of the individual 4,000-meter pursuit (mean time 303.1 seconds). Two cyclists had three samples drawn, one cyclist gave two samples, and four cyclists gave one sample.

The blood lactate values are recorded in millimoles per liter of blood (mM/l), which is how they are reported in scientific literature. (A mole is a given amount of chemical compound by weight. The weight depends upon the number and kind of atoms making up the compound.) A resting value for blood lactate is 1-2mM/l, and values as high as 25-30mM/l have been recorded after exhaustive exercise.

Kilometer produces most

The results for the various events are shown in Table 1. The highest mean value for lactic acid, 16.94mM/l, occurred in the kilometer, an event which requires approximately 70 seconds of all-out riding.

Small differences were found among the events. There was a tendency

	Rest	**Team Pursuit**	**Match Sprints**	**Individual Pursuit**	**Kilometer**
Number of cyclists	4	5	7	12	6
Mean lactate concentration (in M/l)	1.95	12.08	13.65	15.18	16.94
Range of value	1.80-2.23	9.79-15.25	11.40-15.11	13.55-17.31	15.69-18.22
Mean time (seconds)		288.	11.	303.1	70.9

TABLE 1

to have lower lactate concentrations after the 4,000-meter team pursuit. Values were higher in the match sprints, the shortest event, and in the individual pursuit, the longest.

Table 2 shows values for subjects who had multiple samples drawn after individual pursuits. A low correlation was found between riding time and lactic acid concentration. In addition, a wide range of concentration (14.58 and 11.40mM/l) was found in one rider after rounds of the match sprints.

You may wonder why there is a relatively large amount of lactic acid in the blood after a match sprint, a race that requires only about 11 seconds of intense riding. Usually in events of approximately 10 seconds, an athlete will use energy stored in the muscle and produce little lactate. After 10 seconds, only minute quatities of ATP and CP remain in the muscle and glucose or glycogen (stored glucose) is broken down to produce ATP. The demand for ATP is so tremendous that not enough oxygen is available to produce it aerobically. Lactic acid results from anaerobic production and then is diffused into the blood.

TABLE 2

Blood lactate concentrations (mM/l) and performance times (sec) for individual cyclists in various rounds of the individual 4,000-meter pursuit.

Cyclist	Round	Blood Lactate	Time
J.B.	Qualifying	13.73	298.8
	Quarter Finals	13.55	298.8
	Final	15.66	298.0
K.L.	Qualifying	14.25	301.3
	Quarter Finals	14.07	301.3
	Semi-Finals	15.99	303.3
D.G.	Qualifying	16.09	301.2
	Quarter Finals	16.13	301.2
P.D.	Qualifying	17.13	314.2
E.H.	Qualifying	14.88	314.0
B.D.	Qualifying	15.93	308.4
G.P.	Qualifying	14.56	308.2

Previous research with athletes has shown that if the work intensity is sufficiently high, lactic acid can be produced within 10 seconds of work. Kinderman points out that the stress involved in high-intensity exercise may cause increased lactic acid levels. This is attributed to the elevated tone of the nervous system and the increased secretion of adrenalin, which promotes the breakdown of glycogen and glucose.

Train for the stress

While we tend to think of match sprints as very short, high-intensity events, remember that the cyclist is on the track for several minutes under tremendous stress. The high adrenalin output probably causes the high lactate levels. In training, the sprint cyclist is advised to ride under the same conditions as in a meet. Research by Soviet scientists has shown better performances by cyclists who face competitive situations many times during the season.

The lower lactic acid values in the team pursuit compared to the other events could be attributed to the short time a rider spends breaking the wind at the front of the pace line. Chester Kyle has considered wind resistance responsible for 80-90% of the energy cost of cycling. For racing cyclists traveling at 48kph, the required mean power output was reduced 29, 32 and 33% respectively. By taking turns at the front, everyone uses less energy and can complete more of the work aerobically.

The low correlation between individual pursuit times and lactic acid concentration (Table 2) indicates that other variables may be important in predicting performance. The last-lap effort, wind direction, and state of aerobic conditioning may play a part in the amount of lactate produced.

It's easy to see that a major contribution to energy production in track events must come from anaerobic metabolism. The kilometer rider should already know that he must spend time developing his anaerobic system. The sprint cyclist may do well to compete often during the season, in order to train the energy system to the effects of high lactic acid levels.

Paced training for the pursuiter will help lower lactic acid levels by allowing him to rely more on the aerobic energy system. The pursuiter needs a good base of aerobic training, with a gradual increase in interval and pace work as the season progresses.

The overload principle is used in pursuit training — for example, sessions of 2,000-3,000 meters at faster than race pace. Allow complete recovery between rides so that lactic acid will be metabolized. Team pursuiters should work on pace, technique and riding in close quarters.

11.
US riders need more speed work

It's something that has been gnawing at me since 1976, when I first watched U.S. road riders unable to match the breakaway speed or sprint of foreign competitors. Though today some Americans are among the best in the world, for others the problem continues. While riders may have have the endurance to ride any major event, some lack the speed when the final crunch comes.

It is my contention that we in America put too much distance in our training, at the expense of speed and technique. The reason has to do with fear and reluctance to deal with speed. For the unknowing cyclist, upping mileage is a lot simpler than working out a balance between speed, technique and distance training.

While road racing is primarily aerobic in nature, it should be remembered that about 5% is anaerobic. In a 100-mile road race lasting four hours and 10 minutes, 5% would be 12.5 minutes. This is a long time to be using anaerobic sources.

For a cyclist to become appreciably faster, he or she must practice cycling faster. If two riders have comparable natural speed, the one who practices sprinting will win. While simple speedwork and sprinting will help, in-depth results come only from training which concentrates on speed. If the sprint, jump, or breakaway speed is to come under a certain physiological load, then this is what training should simulate.

Note, however, that no high-intensity training should be done without a firm base of conditioning miles. This is especially critical for young people. The following programs can be used to increase cycling speed and develop a powerful jump.

Speed training

An excellent workout consists of a 60km ride with 12km of intervals. First, warm up for 10km at 25kph. Then perform the following intervals

The skill to win a close final sprint comes only from training which concentrates on speed.

during the next 40km before riding the final 10km easy: 1500 meters; 1400; 1300; 1200; 1100; 1000; 900; 800; 700; 600; 500; 400; 300; 200.

All the intervals are performed at maximal speed. Juniors and riders not in top shape should start at 1000 meters. Rest periods between intervals should consist of riding at 30kph until the respiration rate returns to normal. The reason for progressively shorter intervals is to keep speed at a maximum.

The following schedule is used by some riders one or two days per week. Rest periods will vary from individual to individual, but speed should stay at about 30kph.

5km warmup; 2x4km with 10-minute rests; 3x2km with 4-minute rests; 4x1km with 2-minute rests; 10x500 meters with 90-second rests; 5km cool down.

Jump training

The coach follows the group of four to six riders on a motorcycle or in a car. Speed should be 30-35kph. On the signal (horn) the riders jump and ride at maximum speed, and on the second signal the jump is over. The group reassembles and continues at 30kph until the next signal. Several jumps can be used each session.

A second method has a group of about 10 riders carefully assuming a single line and moving at a brisk pace. The last man pulls out and sprints to get to the front, easing up in time to avoid going too far ahead. Every rider must clearly understand that the pace of the group must be maintained, not increased. It must be possible for the last man to be able to reach the front with his sprint. Should he misjudge and go beyond the front man, the latter should avoid the temptation to increase speed to close the gap. On the contrary, he should carefully hold the pace and allow the gap to close gradually. This workout provides jump training, pace judgment and tolerance to the bursts of maximal effort so often demanded in road and criterium racing.

A training program must simulate competition. Cyclists should design their workouts to reflect this basic axiom.

12.
Blood tests
reveal overtraining

Staleness, chronic fatigue, overtraining — it's all the same thing: disaster for the racing cyclist. The crucial task is to find the optimum work level in training and not go beyond. Now blood tests can tell when the danger of overtraining is present and then safely passed.

Overtraining can strike any cyclist who is eager to excel and begins working out frequently with intensity. At first the rider will improve, but ultimately performance will stagnate. The rider tries to pass the sticking point by training even harder. Instead of improving, however, he begins to do worse. A sense of inadequacy and frustration develops and causes changes in his personality and behavior. The same symptoms may occur in a rider who is pushed too fast by his or her coach, or who attends an intensive training camp.

Signs of physiological staleness are weight loss, decrease in strength, fatigue, elevated pulse rate, sallow skin, muscle tenderness, and poor eating and sleeping habits. Psychological symptoms are low interest in training and competition, decreased drive, slump in morale, boredom and nervousness.

To combat the physical roadblocks and maintain a constant interest in riding, vary your training routine, take short layoffs, change environment occasionally and/or take up a different activity for part of the year.

Recently, coaches have begun to use the East German method of monitoring training programs. Frequent testing of the cyclists' blood can spot infection and fatigue before they adversely affect performance. Blood tests help determine a rider's general state of health and training. If abnormalities are present, changes can be made in diet, rest and exercise.

Constituents of blood

The blood constituents used in the evaluation and identification of overtraining are:

Red Blood Cells These supply oxygen to working cells and remove waste products. After a blood sample is taken, these cells are counted and analyzed for size and shape. The normal number for males is 4-6 million; females have slightly less. Low values are seen when there is anemia, severe infection or loss of blood. High values indicate dehydration or certain kidney diseases.

Hemoglobin This is the iron protein substance located within red blood cells. Its primary function is to transport oxygen from the lungs to body tissues. Serum hemoglobin increases when red blood cells are destroyed and a high count indicates certain blood ailments, such as sickle cell disease. Low levels occur after a large blood loss, and sometimes as a result of intensive training. Normal hemoglobin levels are 14-18 grams in men and 12-15 grams in women.

Hematocrit This is the percentage of blood cells (mostly red) in the total blood volume. A blood sample is centrifuged to force solid matter to the bottom of a specially marked tube, leaving clear plasma in the upper section. The test measures the thickness of the blood as well as the amount of fluid in the blood. Low values are seen in cases of excessive fluid intake, severe bleeding, and red blood cell anemia. High concentrations of red cells can occur after exercise in hot weather because sweating causes loss of fluid from the plasma. Normal values are 45-55% in men and slightly lower in women.

White Blood Cells These increase in number when the body is fighting infections or inflammations; the cells help destroy the causative agents. A count includes five types of white blood cells, which are formed and stored in the bone marrow, lymph glands and spleen. The normal range is 5,000-10,000. Emotional stress can raise the white cell count, so a person should be as relaxed as possible before the blood drawing.

Blood tests can be performed on the referral of a physician at any hospital or clinic. To get the most accurate results, rest at least one day after a hard training session or race, and drink enough liquids to be at normal body weight. While a blood test is somewhat expensive ($15 or more), it is a worthwhiles part of your preseason physical. Anytime you go through an extended bad period during the season, a test can help determine the reason.

Blood's role in exercise

The constituents of blood are critical to cycling performance. Since hemoglobin carries oxygen, it is obvious that the number of red blood cells and the amount of hemoglobin in those cells help determine how much oxygen can be supplied to working muscles. Blood also carries away lactic acid, carbon dioxide, and other products of metabolism.

It is not easy to predict the changes in blood after a single bout of cycling or a period of training. There is a wide range of normal at rest values for most blood constituents. The ranges increase with exercise because of variations in training programs and different methods of blood analysis. The bottom line is that athletes do not respond to exercise in the same manner. Their test results should be compared only to their own normal values.

With the above in mind, let's look into some of the research that has dealt with changes in blood chemistry during exercise, training and overtraining.

Hemoglobin a key

The symptoms of overtraining are associated with a decrease in hemoglobin; there seems to be a positive relationship between hemoglobin concentration and performance. Hemoglobin and total blood volume (cells and fluid portion) will vary with the amount and type of training, but athletes should have hemoglobin values comparable to the average population [1-4].

Working with runners, Brotherhood [5] found a significant increase in blood volume and hemoglobin content with no apparent increase in hemoglobin concentration. This may explain the average or sometimes below average hemoglobin concentrations seen in cyclists. But despite a low hemoglobin *concentration,* an athlete may have an average or even above average hemoglobin *content* (hemoglobin concentration divided by body weight).

For example, an athlete may increase total blood volume by 25%, which amounts to about one quart. At the same time, total hemoglobin may be increased to a lesser degree, say 20%. That additional quart or so of blood, therefore, makes the total blood volume slightly thinner than normal in terms of hemoglobin content.

The ability to perform aerobic exercise increases with the percentage of hematocrit, but then begins to decline after a certain level. Too many red blood cells increase the viscosity of blood and put additional stress on the circulatory system.

For example, when blood was drawn from 14 female swimmers within two weeks of the Mexico City Olympics, five showed values below 14.6 grams of hemoglobin and had hematocrits of less than 45%. Of these, four were eliminated in the first heat of their event. The other reached the final of the 200-meter freestyle, in which she finished seventh. By comparison, of the nine whose hematocrit and hemoglobin tested out above these levels, only two were eliminated in the first heat [1].

However, we must be careful in attributing low hemoglobin and hematocrit values in women solely to exercise. In a group of young Olympic athletes in training, 25% of the women were iron deficient and anemic, and another 15% had low serum iron levels without anemia {1}. This "latent" iron deficiency was thought to be secondary to the increased blood cell production seen in athletes, but obviously menstrual loss of iron could contribute to this. It may not be necessary to give premenopausal women cyclists regular iron supplements {6}.

Can diet or food supplements increase hemoglobin content? Shiraki {7} found that "sports anemia" was prevented by increasing the daily intake of protein to as much as 2 grams per kilogram of body weight. Australian athletes had protein intakes of 1.8g/kg/day for males and 1.9 for females. The National Research Council, on the other hand, recommends 0.8g/kg/day for males and females {8}. The question remains open whether or not hemoglobin and red blood cell values are related to intake of protein.

Physical exertion has a rapid effect on circulating white blood cells, causing an increase both after short-term {9, 10} and endurance exercise {11}. Short-term exercise results in lymphocytosis (increase in a type of white blood cell that is active in fighting infections). Endurance exercise causes minimal lymphocytosis but leads to an increase in circulating granulocytes (white blood cells formed in bone marrow).

Tapering

Tapering is the term used for a decrease in the training load in order to rest and ensure a good competitive performance. You can also taper your workouts whenever you begin to feel overtrained.

Can a cyclist be monitored during the tapering phase to ensure optimal performance in major competitions? The answer seems to be "yes." Rushall and Busch {12} studied nine elite male swimmers during a period of hard training, tapering and rest. They looked for changes in hematocrit and hemoglobin. During the hard training period there were 11 workouts each week totaling 11,000-13,000 meters per day. Blood was drawn twice a week and these observations were made:

— Illness and heavy training had a detrimental effect on both hemoglobin and hematocrit values. During the period of hard work, hemoglobin values were below those recorded for males in general.

— All swimmers had a recovery in hemoglobin during the taper phase of their training.

— Of seven swimmers who were measured after competition (following the taper), six recorded values higher than while in the taper.

— The correlation between hemoglobin and hematrocrit was moderate to low; it was concluded that hematocrit was a less sensitive index of response to training.

—Results of blood testing need to be judged on an individual basis, since the swimmers exhibited a wide range of values.

This study shows a decrease in hemoglobin during hard training, with hemoglobin recovery being a good index of the athlete's recovery. Because of such fluctuations, an athlete's hemoglobin count may be misleading if it is compared with that of the average male population.

Summary

In cyclists and other endurance athletes:

Overtraining is a real phenomenon in cyclists and other endurance athletes. Measurement of various blood chemistries and counts can be useful in determining the onset of overtraining and recovery from it.

Below normal hemoglobin and hematocrit values are common in athletes and usually do not reflect true anemia. Response to training is an individual thing. These values must be compared with those of the same athlete when he or she is well rested.

Extensive blood work-ups are not needed if the athlete is performing well.

13.
Winter riding can be bearable

Just thinking about training when it's cold and windy may discourage you from cycling in winter. But with appropriate adjustments for the climate, training during this season can be both beneficial and enjoyable.

When adequately protected, humans can tolerate temperatures between -50 and 210° Fahrenheit, but they can only withstand several degrees of variation in body core temperature. The most important physiologic adjustment to the cold is the maintenance of body temperature. Cycling at slow speed raises body metabolism to an adequate level to maintain body temperature in subzero weather.

In addition, reduced peripheral blood flow from constriction of surface blood vessels and lower skin temperature greatly increases the insulative capacity of the body. These adjustments effectively minimize heat loss at lower ambient temperatures.

During the first few days of very cold weather, you will be bothered more by the cold than after a few weeks. Your body acclimates to the cold by producing increased amounts of heat.

To become accustomed to the cold, you must exercise in the cold. Research has shown that after six weeks of exercise in the cold, exposing the fingers for four hours to cold results in less temperature drop, less numbness, and less restricted blood flow.

It is well known that athletes going from a cold to hot climate must be careful of heat stress during the first week to 10 days. On the other hand, athletes who come from a hot climate to a cold one will be able to exercise hard right away if they take proper precautions.

Temperature is not all that determines the harshness of a winter day. There are limits to sensible and useful winter cycling. The windchill index probably is the best guide. The accompanying chart shows the relative danger at various windchill levels.

TABLE 1

Wind-Chill Chart

Air Temperature (Degrees Fahrenheit)

Wind Speed (M.P.H.)	+50	+40	+30	+20	+10	0	-10	-20
	Adapted from: ENCYCLOPEDIA OF ATHLETIC MEDICINE							
5	48	37	27	16	6	-5	-15	-26
10	40	28	16	4	-9	-24	-33	-46
15	36	22	9	-5	-18	-32	-45	-58
20	32	18	4	-10	-25	-39	-53	-67
25	30	16	0	-15	-29	-44	-59	-74
30	28	13	-2	-18	-33	-48	-63	-79
35	27	11	-4	-20	-35	-51	-67	-82
40	26	10	-6	-21	-37	-53	-69	-85

LITTLE DANGER   INCREASING DANGER   GREAT DANGER

I suggest you do not cycle if the windchill is in the "great danger" zone. In "increasing danger," dress with special care. In "little danger," cycle without fear.

Wind direction is critical. A side wind has a fraction of the impact of a headwind. The trailing wind is important only if you have to return into it. Worth noting, too, is that to ride into the wind at, say, 5mph increases windchill appreciably. A glance at the chart will show that this increment can easily push you out of mild into real danger.

On very bad days you can split your workout up into two shorter rides. Shelterbelts such as trees, buildings, and gullies can considerably modify wind speed so that you may be able to continue longer on your ride.

Many cyclists are concerned about the harmful effects of breathing cold air on lung tissue, but studies have shown that the possibility of damage to pulmonary tissue is extremely remote. When -25°F air is inhaled, it is warmed to 80-90 °F by the time it reaches the lungs. Uncomfortable sensations in the upper respiratory tract probably result from extreme dryness of cold air, which may cause temporary irritation. If you find that breathing cold air makes you feel uncomfortable, wear one of the face masks that goes over your mouth and nose. These masks are porous enough to let air go in and out, and solid enough to help you retain heat and moisture. If your eyes bother you, wear ski goggles for good insulation over the upper face and forehead.

Clothing is crucial to the cyclist in the cold. Though few people know it, the head is the most efficient portion of the body's heating system. If you leave your head unprotected, even in minor wind, you may lose up to one half your body's total heat production. There's truth in the old mountaineer's maxim: when your feet are cold, put on your hat.

Wear mittens, not gloves. Mittens are much warmer than gloves for the simple reason that they trap all the hand's warmth in a single compartment.

Shoe covers are essential to keep the feet dry on damp rides. In addition to the covers, wear heavy socks and try to use all-leather cycling shoes. The mesh type will not help you maintain body warmth.

Wear "condition-variable" clothing that allows you to maintain body temperature over a wide range of conditions. A long-sleeve, zipper-front jacket with attached hood has great variability. When the wind is howling in your face, zip the front and use the hood over your hat. If you begin to get hot, you can make two adjustments (zipper and hood) that will allow you to release the build-up of heat.

What's the best way to dress for comfort on your winter ride? Wear several layers of clothing. The layer next to the skin should reduce evaporative heat loss by wicking away sweat. Try using acrylic or a wool blend as the inner garment. A middle layer of wool, polyester or pile will insulate well. The top layer should block both wind and water. Good materials are nylon, polyester and wool. Gore-Tex is a new material that breathes but stops penetration of wind and water. Long-sleeve wool or wool-blend jerseys with nylon on the front are also effective at blocking wind while preventing excessive build-up of body heat.

Even with the best precautions, hypothermia may occur. Hypothermia arises when the core temperature of the body is lowered through exposure and exhaustion.

Hypothermia can happen to the cyclist at temperatures well above freezing if the proper conditions of cold, wet and wind are present. If you begin to shiver on the ride, either work harder until the shivering stops or go home. Dry yourself and change into dry clothes as soon as possible. Then cover yourself with warm blankets. Take in hot liquids and warm foods, especially carbohydrates. If the symptoms do not subside, have someone get in touch with a physician immediately.

A useful reminder in winter cycling is VIP: Ventilate, Insulate, Protect. Ventilate excess water for perspiration. Insulate, particularly high blood flow areas like the head and neck. Protect from wind and wetness with appropriate clothing.

For many of us, the hardest part of winter cycling is getting started. Conditions may appear colder outside than they are once you get under way. Your body turns out enough heat to keep you warm if you'll only help out a little.

14.
Use plyometrics
to increase strength

A strength training program that is now being used in various sports has applications to cycling. It's called plyometrics.

Plyo . . . what? Plyometrics, simply defined, is a series of drills that place muscles in a prestretched position before they shorten (concentric contraction). The results are said to be improved strength, speed and explosive power.

Plyometric training overloads the muscles via jumping movements. When you land from a jump (figure 1), the muscles tense while lengthening to a prestretched position (eccentric contraction). This is followed immediately by an explosive concentric contraction. The goal is to simulate the movements and speed of contraction seen during competition.

If you have difficulty visualizing this, think of a rubber band and how it responds to stretch. When you increase the stretch, tension and the velocity of shortening become greater. Muscle has structure of contractile and elastic components, each involved in the development of force. When the elastic component is stretched, tension is produced.

Muscles have stretch receptors. Invoking the stretch reflex of a muscle in combination with a voluntary contraction results in a more vigorous contraction. In plyometrics, a muscle's elastic component and stretch reflex contribute to the total force generated in a contraction.

Plyometrics testing

The ability of plyometrics to increase strength and power has been proven in tests. In a study with collegiate football players, one group used plyometric drills (jumping from a height of 45cm) in combination with weight training. A control group did only conventional weight training exercises. After six weeks the group using plyometrics had greater gains in strength.

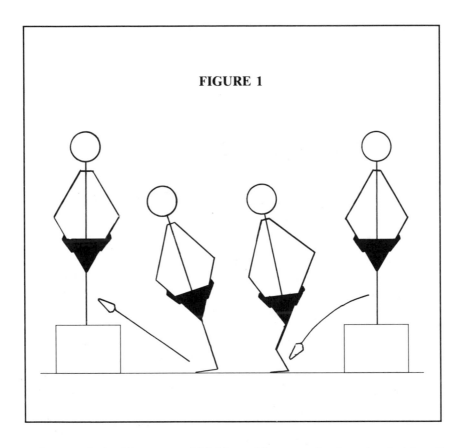

FIGURE 1

In a study by Blattner and Noble, subjects used a jumping height of 34 inches and gradually added weight (using a weight vest) up to 20 lbs. After eight weeks there was an increase of more than two inches in vertical jump, a 10% improvement.

Training progressions

Plyometrics can be applied like weight training, using the overload principle by progressively increasing
— number of repetitions
— number of sets
— height of jumping block
— weight in weight vest

As with any training program, the athlete's age must be considered. A mature cyclist usually can handle rigorous workouts. An Intermediate or Junior may wish to use plyometrics only in the off season, while a

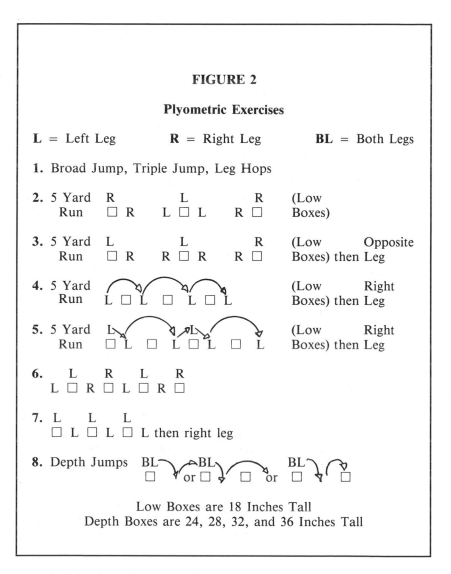

FIGURE 2

Plyometric Exercises

L = Left Leg   **R** = Right Leg   **BL** = Both Legs

1. Broad Jump, Triple Jump, Leg Hops

Low Boxes are 18 Inches Tall
Depth Boxes are 24, 28, 32, and 36 Inches Tall

Senior can use it year-round. The biggest concern is the overloading of thigh muscles, which may lead to knee pain.

Plyometrics is best suited for cyclists who need to develop power, speed and acceleration. Those who compete in the kilometer, match sprint, pursuit and possibly 100-kilometer team time trial can expect significant improvement from a progressive plyometric program. The long-distance road specialist may wish to use it only in the off season.

Training programs

Figure 2 shows various plyometric exercises appropriate for cyclists. During the first three weeks, limit the workout to broad jumps, triple jumps, single leg hops and jumps off low boxes. Work out twice a week, doing no more than 60 jumping movements (repetitions) per session.

After three weeks, increase the sessions to every other day and the repetitions to 75-85. Incorporate a variety of hopping exercises, for example: 1) right leg, left, right, left, etc. as in exaggerated running; 2) right, right, left, left, etc.; 3) all right leg or all left. Do these hops for 30 yards at full speed. Add jumps from boxes 14-24 inches high. This phase should last about four weeks.

After one month, you can increase the height of the boxes and wear a weighted vest. Do not use ankle weights — they are too hard on the feet and ankles. Add bounding up stairs to the program. The maximum number of repetitions per workout should be 100.

Keep your hands on your hips during all these exercises. Using the arms is cheating and takes away from the work of the legs.

Once the racing season arrives, you can continue to do one or possibly two plyometric sessions per week, depending on your needs. Track cyclists can do their plyometrics in the infield between sessions on the bike.

Summary

In designing and using a plyometrics program, remember:

1. Warm up well before beginning heavy exertion.

2. Stretch the muscles quickly to develop maximum tension — the faster the prestretch the greater the tension.

3. Follow the principle of overloading when developing your program.

Plyometric exercise is a good way to develop strength and power. It can make a significant contribution to those who lack an ergometer and weights, or simply wish to add variety to their winter training routine.

15.
Next season starts now with weights, ergometer

December is when you need to start a training schedule which will have you at maximum physical peak by the time the important races arrive. Early season training should emphasize total body conditioning and an increase in muscular strength over the prior season.

Circuit training has become popular in the last few years. This is a scientific arrangement of exercises intended to develop all-around fitness. You perform specific exercises at various stations, usually within a limited period of time. At the conclusion of one exercise you move rapidly to the next station; once the exercises at all the stations have been done the circuit is complete.

The exercises usually involve weight resistance, but running, stationary cycling, calisthenics and stretching may also be included. Circuit training can be designed to increase muscular strength, endurance, flexibility and cardiovascular fitness.

The circuit should include exercises that will develop your total body, with emphasis on the muscular groups used in cycling. There are usually between 10 and 15 stations, one circuit of which requires 10 to 20 minutes to complete. You perform several circuits during the workout, with 15 seconds rest between stations.

At eight resistance stations, the weight should be such that your muscles are fatigued after performing as many repetitions as possible within a designated time period (e.g. 30 seconds). Add more weight when you notice a significant rise in repetitions. Arrange the stations so that the same muscle group is not being exercised consecutively. Continue this program until the season begins.

An example of a circuit program for cycling follows. Though you may not be able to design an identical circuit, be innovative and set up a program to fit the available resources.

Station	Exercise
1	Bicycle ergometer (3 min)
2	Bent knee sit-ups
3	Bent over rowing
4	Dead lift
5	Knee extension
6	Arm curl
7	Bicycle ergometer (3 min)
8	Upright rowing
9	Leg curl (knee flexion)
10	Bench press
11	Back hyperextension
12	Calf raises

Circuits per session — two or three
Weight load — 40% to 55% of one maximum repetition
Repetitions — as many as possible in 30 seconds
Rest — 15 seconds between exercises
Frequency — two or three sessions per week

A circuit using a Universal Gym is excellent because it's easy to change the weight quickly. But you don't need expensive equipment, and the circuit can be set up in a basement or garage. If you don't have an ergometer, incorporate a 440-660-yard run into the program. Any good program will help develop muscular strength, endurance and cardiovascular fitness.

For track riders

The success of East German and Soviet cyclists in the last several years has prompted much interest in strength programs for the track cyclist.

American coaches and riders are interested in the reasons behind such dramatic improvements. Greater knowledge of the science of coaching, and a more sophisticated approach in training techniques for elite cyclists are responsible for much of the East European progress.

Strength and anaerobic endurance are two of the fundamental requirements of the track rider. To increase the speed of a cyclist, one or both of the speed components — pedal cadence and stroke intensity — must be developed. Since most cyclists seem to have no trouble increasing pedal speed, they must work on strength.

Following are some basic weight resistance exercises for a track cyclist.

World 500- and 1,000-meter record holder Rory O'Reilly knows that winter weight work pays off in summer strength.

Many of these exercises can be performed with free weights or a Universal Gym. The rate of execution of the exercise is important; the weight used should allow 1-12 proper lifts per minute.

UPPER BODY — 1. Bench press; 2. Bent arm pullover; 3. Upright rowing; 4. Hyperextension; 5. Bent over rowing; 6. Lateral pulldown; 7. Bicep curl; 8. Tricep curl; 9. Wrist curl; 10. Reverse wrist curl; 11. Bent knee sit-up.

LOWER BODY — 1. Squat; 2. Leg extension; 3. Leg curl; 4. Calf raise; 5. Leg press; 6. Bicycle ergometer.

Ergometer workout

Coaches and cyclists are quickly learning that the bicycle ergometer is excellent as a strength and power training device. It can improve your jump to maximum pedal speed, develop your ATP-PC system, lactic acid system and staying power. But training on an ergometer is very exhausting. You should allow adequate rest between repetitions and workouts.

Listed below are four routines designed to improve your force output. Work into the program slowly and then increase the repetitions as your fitness grows. Many a naive cyclist has worked himself into a state of chronic fatigue by not following a progressive and organized program. Warm up properly before every ergometer training session and follow with a cool-down period.

1. Jump training. Set the resistance to near maximum and try to reach maximum speed from a full stop as soon as possible. Then hold it for approximately 20 seconds. Repeat eight to 12 of these in a workout. Allow at least 90 seconds of easy pedaling between repetitions to permit the store of high energy fuel (ATP-CP) in your muscles to be replenished.

2. Sprint training. While pedaling, adjust the resistance to maximum and keep cranking until your cadence drops below 90 or 100. Do this eight to 12 times per workout, allowing the same recovery time as in jump training.

3. Lactic acid training. Do intervals of 60-90 seconds to improve your body's physiological ability to work anaerobically and to tolerate lactic acid buildup. Complete 8 to 10 per workout. Rest intervals should consist of easy pedaling for about three minutes. Work at 85-95% of maximum.

4. Staying power (anaerobic endurance). Do intervals of two to three minutes at about 85% of maximum. Do four to six repetitions per workout with relief periods of about four minutes.

Strength training should be done two times per week after the cyclist has had several weeks of general conditioning. Upper body work should continue to be done once a week during the competitive season, ceasing only seven to 10 days before a major championship period (During this short time there will not be any major loss of muscular strenth).

The above weight training and ergometer programs are very intense and the beginning cyclist or Junior should lower the times or totals somewhat. The best program for you is one that fits your ability.

16.
How much protein do you need?

A cyclist's daily diet normally is composed of 45% carbohydrates, 30-40% fat and 15-20% protein. At the training table, however, I often hear coaches tell cyclists to eat more protein during periods of strenuous riding. Is this necessary, or is normal protein consumption adequate for all conditions?

Energy for muscular work comes from two major nutrients, carbohydrates and fat. Very little energy (1-4%) is derived from protein except in unusual circumstances, such as extended fasting or a high-protein, low-carbohydrate diet. However, protein is necessary to make enzymes (the catalysts necessary for all metabolic processes), as well as some hormones, antibodies, and plasma proteins, which carry nutrients and help prevent water from leaving the blood in excessive quantities.

While a child is growing and new tissue is forming, there is a greater need for protein than after he reaches physical maturity. Therefore Intermediates and Juniors should include a higher percentage of protein in their diets than adults.

Amino acids are the structural units of protein. There are 22 amino acids (19 are found in foods) and they are divided into two groups, essential and nonessential. An essential amino acid is necessary for growth and development. It must come from food. A nonessential amino acid can be produced by the body. Of the 10 essential amino acids, two are needed for growth during infancy and childhood, but they are not essential during adulthood. Therefore, for an adult there are eight essential amino acids.

Proteins are classified as complete or incomplete. The former contain all the essential amino acids while the latter are missing one or more. Complete proteins include milk, eggs, dairy products, meat, fish and poultry. Incomplete proteins include grains, vegetables and nuts.

Although carbohydrates and fats provide the energy for muscular work, protein is necessary for muscle growth and development.

In a diet containing both animal and plant protein, there is virtually no risk of missing essential amino acids. In a vegetarian diet derived mostly from plants, the incomplete proteins must be combined in order to provide all the essential amino acids. It is important that this combining take place because complete proteins must be consumed at each meal in order for protein synthesis to proceed. Synthesis will not occur unless all the necessary amino acids are present.

The recommended dietary allowance (RDA) for protein, based on a mixed diet (animal and plant sources) is 0.8 grams per kilogram of body weight per day. For a 150-pound (68kg) cyclist, this equals 54 grams per day. Considering that the RDA has a built-in margin of safety, and that muscular development requires a relatively small amount of additional protein, many nutritional scientists say that the RDA for protein is sufficient for athletes in vigorous training and development.

According to statistics, the average daily protein intake is 89 grams for an American 12-17 years old. It is 111 grams for 18-44-year-olds. Some studies indicate that athletes consume 150-400 grams per day.

TABLE 1
Protein Content of Various Food Groups

Food Type	Quantity	Grams/Protein
Egg	1	7
Meat, fish, poultry	3 ounces	20-27
Milk	1 cup	8
Cheese	1 ounce	7-8
Peanut Butter	2 tablespoons	7-8
Peanuts	2 tablespoons	6-7
Bread	1 slice	2-3
Fruit	1 cup	1
Vegetables	1 cup	4
Pasta	1 cup	4-6
Pizza	1 piece (medium)	8-10

What happens to excess protein if it is not used for growth and development? It is broken down into nitrogen and byproducts. The nitrogen is then excreted in the urine while nonnitrogen products are either converted to carbohyrates or fat and used for energy production, or they are stored as fat.

The sprinter or kilometer rider who wants to increase muscle mass should take care not to gain fat instead. Rapid weight gain usually indicates an increase in fat, not lean body mass.

In order to calculate your daily intake it is important to know serving size and protein content. The table gives examples of protein content for several basic foods. Record your meals for several days to get a picture of your protein consumption. Check at a bookstore or your library for a book with a more extensive table.

It appears that the best advice for most competitive cyclists is to eat a balanced diet with a protein intake at the RDA level. A variety of foods will ensure that all nutrients are consumed, including the essential amino acids.

17.
Problems with milk products

We have heard many times that carbohydrates are the most efficient energy food for cyclists. While glucose and sucrose are the most common carbohydrates, lactose, found in milk and certain milk products, is another.

However, lactose and milk have been held responsible for a number of ill effects experienced by some cyclists. The amount of milk that will cause trouble varies. It might be a couple of ounces — hardly more than you would put in your coffee or cereal — or it might be a glass or more. Problems include abdominal cramping, mild diarrhea, "cottonmouth," flatulence and general discomfort {1}.

Lactose is virtually the only carbohydrate in cow's milk and constitutes 4-5% of milk's total weight. Lactose is broken down into simple sugars (glucose and galactose) by the enzyme lactase, which is located in the cells lining the intestinal wall. Cyclists intolerant to milk do not have lactase in their systems. The lactose, therefore, does not get absorbed readily into the bloodstream and remains in the intestine, drawing in fluids and causing a large volume of liquid stool that has to get out. In the middle of a long ride, the discomfort can be intense.

The ability to digest lactose varies both among individuals and races of people. Africans, Asiatics, a majority of blacks and about 10% of the North American white population are found to suffer from lactose-related complaints. Why should this racial difference exist? The answer is obscure, and researchers are divided in their opinions as to whether the difference is genetic or environmental. Either we inherit the inability to digest lactose normally or we develop it by failing to drink enough milk after weaning. This dietary deficiency during early years could cause the level of the enzyme lactase to decrease in the intestine {2}.

If you have symptoms that indicate milk intolerance, how can you tell for sure? One way is to have a lactose-intolerance test. You consume a specified amount of milk (or lactose) and have blood samples taken every few minutes for an hour. If you have plenty of lactase, the blood will contain high levels of blood sugar because the lactase is adequate to break down the lactose in the intestine. Conversely, low blood sugar levels point to lactose intolerance.

Another way is to keep a food diary. Record the foods you eat, and you may be able to see recurring problems each time you consume milk products. Read labels on foods to be certain whether the ingredients include milk or milk derivatives. If you suspect lactose intolerance, consult your physician for further testing and advice on a lactose-free diet.

Cyclists who have lactose intolerance can usually eat some milk products. Yogurt, hard cheeses and similar dairy products have their milk sugar digested by bacterial action and can be eaten comfortably. There is a product available at most supermarkets, Lact-Aid, that can be added to milk. It is made from yeast and provides the missing or deficient enzyme.

Some coaches urge even cyclists tolerant to milk to restrict it before training and particularly in the pre-race meal. They say that milk could contribute to the development of upset stomach and cottonmouth. However, one investigation conducted on endurance athletes found no scientific evidence that milk hampered performance capacity {3}. Indeed, when milk products are eliminated from the diet, nutrients such as calcium and riboflavin might fall below recommended levels. In reviewing the literature and conducting his own research, Nelson concluded that if an athlete likes milk and wants it in his pre-game meal, there is no reason to eliminate it {4}.

The contention that milk will cause cottonmouth is unfounded. Cottonmouth is usually the result of tension, which causes the salivary glands to decrease the flow of saliva. As a result, the mouth becomes dry. Water, ice, soft drinks and chewing gum are often effective in combating this condition {5}.

All cyclists should include some dairy products in their daily diet. If you are one of those who cannot digest milk, try other dairy products in which the lactose has been either removed or altered through fermentation.

18.
Helps and hazards of steroid use

The expulsion of athletes (including a Chilean cyclist) from the Pan American Games brought the use of anabolic steroids to public notice. A story on drugs in *Sports Illustrated* included a photo of Joop Zoetemelk and stated that he was penalized for steroid use.

With the known penalties for steroid use and the possible side effects associated with its prolonged use, why do we see a continued and possible increased use by athletes?

The answer may be in the following remarks of a world-class athlete. "Think about how small the differences are usually between first and second place, between winning and losing, and keep in mind the drive and ambition and competitive spirit of somebody competing at that level. Think about the time, the energy, and the pain invested. . . . The financial rewards are, in most cases, minimal. . . . I hate to admit it, but an obsessive-compulsive personality is practically a requirement (for success at these levels). . . . The average guy on the street, and even lots of people in sports obviously don't understand the pressures. . . . It's like everything else in life; when it all gets down to the nitty-gritty, you grab anything you can that might give you a winning edge." [1]

With drive and ambition like this, is it any wonder that athletes would take steroids to improve performance?

Anabolic steroids are synthetic derivatives of the natural male steroid hormone, testosterone. Anabolic refers to hormones which promote tissue growth, increased muscle mass, increased hemoglobin concentration, without the concurrent development of the secondary male sexual characteristics.

These hormones stimulate protein synthesis. They are used to treat such diverse diseases as osteoporosis, anorexia nervosa, breast cancer and a wide variety of anemias. They also promote healing in the cases of severe burns, fractures, surgery, infectious diseases or general run-down condition, all of which occur in people of both sexes and all ages.

Research indicates that anabolic steroids in high doses combined with heavy resistance training will result in an increase in body weight and muscle size. This increase in an athlete's body weight is the result of an increase in both body water and lean body mass.

There is certainly a behavioral effect associated with steroids. When athletes come off them, they feel depressed. When they're on them they think they train more aggressivley and, in fact, many do. Individual responses to different steroids vary widely. Athletes shop around and try different brands to see which are most effective {2}.

Because of possible increases in strength, you can see why sprinters and kilometer riders would use these products. But why are positive tests showing up with road cyclists?

The answer lies in the effect of steroids on the blood. Anabolic steroids taken in therapeutic and supratherapeutic doses increase the absolute red cell mass over a treatment period of a few weeks. Initially, there may be no change in the hemoglobin concentrate, but the actual blood volume may increase more than 15% above normal volume. If the steroid is discontinued, the extra plasma volume will be swiftly restored to a pretreatment level and leave the increased red blood cell mass, resulting in an increased hemoglobin concentration.

Therefore, steroids can increase maximal aerobic capacity by increasing the blood's ability to deliver oxygen to the working muscle. The increased level of red blood cells and elevated hemoglobin concentration may persist for several weeks after taking steroids {3}. Is it any wonder with the ability to increase aerobic potential, endure more work and increase aggressiveness that a stage race cyclist may use anabolic steroids? What, then, are the hazards associated with steroid use? Side effects of anabolic steroids are serious. Edema associated with sodium retention occurs with all these drugs, and accounts for at least a portion of the desired weight gain. Increased secretion of the sebaceous glands can lead to acne, especially in women. Disturbances in the excretory function of the liver may also occur. In addition, there have been reports of liver cancer associated with long term steroid use {4}. Other side effects may include nausea, loss of appetite, and increased or decreased sexual drive. A sequel to steroid use in women will also be the development of male secondary sexual characteristics. These changes are not masked by the concurrent use of estrogens, and in many cases are not reversible even when steroids are discontinued.

The pressures on our athletes are increasingly tremendous. Is the cost of using anabolic steroids or any drug worth the price of victory?

19.
Things you should know about DMSO

DMSO — dimethyl sulfoxide — has been used to treat everything from tendinitis to muscle tears and ankle sprains. It came to national attention a few years ago when arthritis victims reported on CBS *60 Minutes* that their pains vanished and they were able to return to normal daily activities after treatment with DMSO.

Though you may find DMSO a useful treatment for certain conditions, there are some things you should know about the drug before trying it.

First synthesized by a Russian scientist in 1866, DMSO is a natural by-product of wood-pulp manufacturing and has been used for decades as an industrial solvent, paint thinner and additive in a number of chemical products. Around 1960 the medical profession found it protected biological tissues from damage when they were preserved by freezing. With further research in the early '60s, DMSO was reported to penetrate skin rapidly, to have a local analgesic activity and to decrease swelling and promote healing.

Alarmed by DMSO's sudden popularity, the Federal Drug Administration conducted research that suggested it caused eye damage in laboratory rats. Several tests performed on rabbits, dogs and pigs indicated that DMSO made the lenses of their eyes dense and left them nearsighted. In '65 the FDA discontinued research and cleared DMSO for treatment of one condition, a bladder inflammation called interstitial cystitis.

The adverse laboratory findings have so far not dampened sales. Open any running magazine and there are advertisements from mail order houses with toll-free numbers where credit cards are accepted for the purchase of industrial-grade DMSO. Industrial-grade is almost twice as potent as the human-use formula, but because it contains many impurities that may be carcinogens (pesticides, for example), it is not recommended for human application.

Human-grade DMSO is manufactured by Research Industries in Utah and can be prescribed by physicians only in the states of Florida and Oregon.

DMSO enters the skin quickly and is absorbed by the blood. Several minutes after it is administered, you will notice the taste of raw oysters or garlic on your breath. When DMSO reaches the lungs it releases dimethyl sulfide which causes the ill-flavored taste. A strong mouthwash will help. Body odor may also develop.

DMSO does not reduce injury-induced swelling after it has occurred but it will prevent swelling if used early enough after an injury. It is thought to replace the fluid that causes pain and swelling around the injured area. When DMSO moves the fluid into the blood, the swelling and pressure supposedly disappear and so does the pain.

Since it passes through the skin quickly, DMSO has also been used as a transfer agent to get medication to an injured site. Crushed aspirin and hydrocortisone cream can be applied topically with DMSO.

Using DMSO is simple if you take several precautions. DMSO works best when used as soon as possible after an injury. Use the human grade and dilute it to 60-65 percent solution with distilled water in a clear container. A more concentrated solution can cause blisters or a rash. Applying DMSO is the tricky part. Thoroughly clean the skin around the injured area. Remember, anything left on the skin will be absorbed into the blood stream. Apply the chemical with a clear Q-tip or clear pad that contains no dyes or coloring. Don't rub too hard or you'll burn your skin. Cover the area with a pad or Saran Wrap and an elastic bandage and leave it covered for several hours. You may feel a tingling sensation but this is nothing to worry about. The lighter your skin the more susceptible you will be to a blister or rash. If this does occur, apply ice or skin cream to the area. Do not wear any dyed clothing directly near the DMSO.

DMSO is apparently not a wonder drug for everyone. Some athletes are simply left with bad breath and pains after using it. Others find it to be no more than a mild analgesic like aspirin. (Since very few control studies have been completed, no one knows whether prolonged use of DMSO may be dangerous.)

The FDA seems willing to approve DMSO, but warns "there is no evidence that DMSO alters the course of any disease or is, in any sense, a miracle drug. To suggest on the basis of the evidence available to date, controlled or uncontrolled, that DMSO is a major medical advance for any serious disease, let alone a variety of such diseases, is misleading."

One reason DMSO has received little attention from researchers and drug companies is because it is cheap to produce and cannot be patented. During the '60s at least three major drug firms considered marketing

DMSO commercially but lost interest. The drug cannot be patented as an original molecule and thus the potential profit is low.

In the meantime, what is the bottom line for the injured cyclist? Is DMSO safe and, if it is, does it improve healing? At present there is no definitive answer, but within the next few years researchers hope to discover whether it is worthless, harmful or a miracle drug.

20.
What happens on trip to dope control?

Cyclists often feel a tremendous amount of pressure to perform to their maximum. Some comes from within and the rest is heaped upon them by friends, family, teammates and coaches. It is not surprising, therefore, that riders are tempted to use drugs to gain an advantage through stimulation, increases in strength or blocking of pain. Coaches and trainers have been known to encourage drug use for these purposes and even provide the substances.

Even though deaths have occurred from the misuse of drugs at all levels of cycling, some people question the need for doping control. They say, "Why shouldn't a rider have the choice of any method of training or any drug despite its potential health danger? If he dies in attempting to excel, it's his responsibility."

One reply is that the use of drugs contravenes a basic characteristic of sport, the matching of strength and skill based on the natural capabilities of the athletes. But beyond this ideal there are the following practical considerations.

Some physicians and coaches place the desire for success above their responsibility for the welfare of the competitors under their care. There have been cases in which drugs were administered to cyclists who were unaware of what they were and what effects they would produce.

The use of some drugs, such as amphetamines, can cause aggression and loss of judgment. A rider may then be a danger to other cyclists, spectators and officials.

It is natural for young riders to emulate the established heroes of the sport. If leading cyclists were allowed to use drugs in competition or training, many others would be sure to do so. (Since 1960 there has been an ongoing crackdown on the problem of drug use by cyclists, and new substances are continually being added to the list of those drugs banned from

Found in coffee, tea and soft drinks, caffeine is an ergogenic aid used by cyclists around the world. As of 1985 the International Olympic Committee has designated it as an illegal substance with a legal limit.

sport. Still each season there are numerous positive findings in post-race urine tests. These medical controls are now part of all major national and international competitions. Every cyclist, coach, manager and physician associated with a team participating in such events should be familiar with how dope testing is conducted.

Selection for testing

The first three finishers and not fewer than two riders selected at random are required to report and submit urine samples after a race.

In stage races, samples must be supplied by the first two to finish the stage, the leader in general classification, and two riders picked at random. After time trial stages the four fastest riders must report and none are drawn by lot.

Notification of riders

If you are selected for medical control, an official will present you with a card soon after the event, usually before the award ceremony. You must sign a copy of the card to indicate that you have received notice. You then have 60 minutes to report.

If you are riding in a second event or are delayed for some reason, a team representative should inform the medical control of your whereabouts. If you do not report you will immediately be banned from racing for one month.

Medical control procedure

Only authorized personnel are allowed in the medical control unit. This includes the physician, officials and male and female chaperones. You should bring your team physician or manager with you.

After signing several forms you will receive two 50ml bottles and one 150ml receptacle. You will be escorted to the laboratory where you must make yourself naked from the middle of your back to your knees. Your sleeves must be rolled up to make treachery impossible. The urine is collected in the large receptacle and divided between the small ones. Each must receive between 35 and 50ml.

An official will close the bottles by either applying a sealing wax or lead seal directly to the stopper. You may also affix your own seal if you wish. Finally a form is signed by all concerned to verify that the full procedure was carried out properly.

If you are unable to urinate you will be kept in the facility for as long as it takes; there is no time limit. Should the doctor permit you to leave for some reason, such as a press interview, an official will stay with you until you are finally able to give a sample.

The collected urine is shipped to the nearest approved lab for tests that will reveal the presence of drugs. Usually the results are ready in 12 to 24 hours.

Positive findings

If the test on the first sample is positive, the urine in the second bottle will be tested in the presence of an expert appointed by the cycling federation of the event's host country. This person must be there when the seal on the bottle is broken and the contents are analyzed. Riders may be represented by their own physicians. A positive finding in the second test cannot be appealed, and the amateur cyclist will receive the following penalties:

1st offense — disqualification and a one-month suspension
2nd offense — disqualification and a three-month suspension
3rd offense — confiscation and non-renewal of license

List of banned drugs

The list of drugs banned by the International Olympic Committee is shown below. At the end of each category there is the phrase "and related compounds." This leaves the door open for the I.O.C. to add any other drugs it decides should be banned.

A physician who views this list will quickly realize that treating the common cold, flu, asthma, etc. with many medications will not be possible when a rider may be subjected to a drug test. Many over-the-counter products like Visine, Contac, and Afrin will also produce positive results. If medication must be administered during the competition, the team doctor should discuss the drug with the official race physician to determine if it is permitted.

Doping control is a time-consuming and expensive procedure, but it must be carried out to guarantee the integrity of the competition. Familiarity with the substances and procedures will mean less chance of inadvertent use of banned drugs, and riders will experience less fear and frustration during the testing procedure.

I.O.C. List of Doping Substances

Psychomotor stimulant drugs — amphetamine, benzphetamine, chlorphentermine, cocaine, diethylpropion, dimethylamphetamine, ethylamphetamine, fencamfamin, meclofenoxate, methylamphetamine, methylphenidate, norpseudoephedrine, pemoline, phendimetrazine, phenmetrazine, phentermine, pipradol, prolintane, and related compounds.

Sympathomimetic amines — chlorprenaline, ephedrine, etafearine, isoetharine, isoprenaline, methylephedrine, methoxyphenamine, and related compounds.

Miscellaneous central nervous system stimulants — amiphenazole, bemigride, doxapram, ethamivan, leptazol, nikethamide, picrotoxin, strychnine, and related compounds.

Anabolic steroids — methandienone, stanozolol, oxymetholone, nandrolone decanoate, nandrolone phenylpropionate, and related compounds.

Narcotic analgesics — anileridine, codeine, dextromoramide, dihydrocodeine, dipipanone, ethylmorphine, heroin, hydrocodone, hydromorphone, levorphanol, methadone, morphine, oxocodone, oxomorphone, pentazocine, pethidine, phenazocine, piminodine, thebacon, trimeperidine, and related compounds.

21.
The preseason physical

The preseason physical examination is important for athletes. Even if you feel in perfect health, the doctor must determine whether you are physically and psychologically fit in all respects to enter into serious training and meet the stress of the upcoming season. The various cardiovascular, neurological, orthopedic and respiratory irregularities that may be discovered need to be treated before the season begins.

Whether performed by your primary physician or by a specialist, the preseason physical should determine the following:

— Any medical or orthopedic problem which would be aggravated by cycling or early season activities, such as weight training

— Any medical or orthopedic problem which requires further evaluation and/or therapy in order for you to perform rigorous exercise

— In young athletes especially, any structural characteristics which predispose to injury and which may require preventive devices, such as orthotics

— The level of physical fitness to see if specific conditioning programs are needed

Finally the exam provides a baseline for later reference in case of an injury.

Several areas of assessment must be performed at least one month before the season starts to allow time for treatment if needed.

Make sure your doctor gets your complete medical and injury history, covering prior and current medical problems, previous injuries, and symptoms related to exercise, such as wheezing or lightheadedness. If you fill out a history form yourself, be sure you understand all the terms used.

Have a complete physical including blood tests and red blood cell, hemoglobin, hematocrit, and white blood cell counts, which establish your general state of health. These are especially useful if you are experiencing chronic problems with training or have symptoms of staleness. The physician can suggest changes in diet, sleep, rest and training if abnormalities exist.

A well conditioned cyclist will not only perform better but will be at less risk for injury. There are several measures of fitness which can tell you if you need to establish a program to improve your conditioning. First is body composition. This can be measured in several ways, the most practical being skinfold calipers. Underwater weighing is more accurate, if you can find a place that does it. Knowing your percent body fat will help you decide on an appropriate diet.

Body flexibility tests measure your maximum range of motion on specific exercises. Tight muscles increase the risk of musculotendinous injury. A preventive stretching program may be needed.

Cardiovascular endurance is assessed by a stress test on a bicycle ergometer. If your endurance is low you will fatigue easily and be more susceptible to injury, as well as suffer diminished performance.

In addition to having a physical exam, you should also make a yearly trip to your dentist and optometrist. Poor eyesight and nagging dental problems will only hinder you in reaching your maximum potential.

22.
Causes and cures of knee injuries

Injuries to the knee are perhaps the most feared in cycling, and with good reason — they are the most common cause of permanent disability in the sport. Knee problems can be caused by any number of factors, including incorrect saddle height, improper cleat position, cold weather, a direct blow in an accident, using too large a gear and inherited foot abnormalities.

Anatomy of a knee

The knee is a simple hinged joint joining the femur bone of the thigh and the tibia bone of the lower leg (Figure 1). As many athletes find out, it is an unstable connection at best, depending on muscle, tendon, ligament and cartilage for added sturdiness.

At the front of the knee joint are the quadriceps muscles, the patella (kneecap) and the patellar tendon. The patella is important in straightening the knee as it transfers the forces created by the quadriceps to the leg. It also helps protect the area from direct blows. The underside of the patella is covered with a smooth, firm cartilage.

The back of the knee is supported by a group of ligaments referred to as the posterior capsule. The inner side is shored up by the medial collateral ligament, while the outer side is bolstered by the lateral collateral ligament (Figure 2).

The inside is stabilized by the anterior and posterior ligaments, which control front-to-back movements. Between the femur and tibia lie two cartilages that provide shock absorption as well as support. Finally, the knee is surrounded by synovial fluid and bursa for lubrication in the spaces between moving parts.

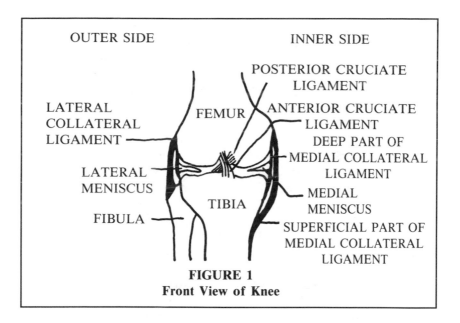

FIGURE 1
Front View of Knee

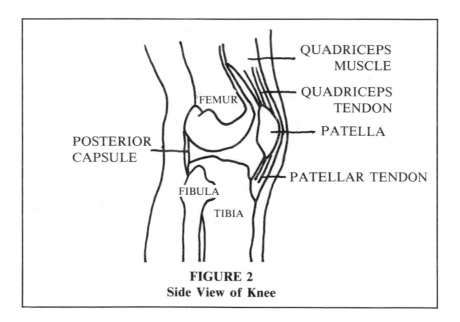

FIGURE 2
Side View of Knee

Chondromalacia

Probably the most disabling knee problem in cycling is chondromalacia. This is often referred to as "runner's knee" because it is an affliction widespread among the country's 30 million or so runners. Basically, the condition is due to a tracking abnormality of the patella as it glides up and down in the groove between the femur and tibia during flexion and extension.

The term chondromalacia means disintegration of the patella and femoral cartilage surfaces. When the patella doesn't ride properly in its groove, the cartilage becomes rough and irregular. Symptoms start with deep knee pain and a grating or crunching sensation in the kneecap. The problem can seem to go away during cycling, only to return at the end of the ride or later in the day.

Chondromalacia is a difficult problem to treat, and there is no satisfactory cure for it. Therefore, it is important to recognize the early signs in order to prevent progression to a chronic injury. Check your saddle height and foot position to make sure the pain isn't being caused by incorrect adjustment. Orthotics (custom supports worn in shoes) can often improve chondromalacia if it is caused by foot abnormalities.

Staying off the bike is essential. Treatment includes rest, aspirin and application of ice to the knee for periods of five to seven minutes. Once the pain is gone and the problem that caused it has been corrected, you can begin exercises which strengthen the quadricep muscles. Strong quads are important in the proper tracking of the patella.

Osgood-Schlatter's disease

Especially in boys aged 10-14, pain can occur in front of and below the knee. It can be aggravated by cycling. The powerful quadriceps attach to the patella and then to the patellar tendon, which is attached to the tibia. In rapidly growing youngsters, this area of the bone is the weakest. When the quadriceps contract and pull the patella and patellar tendon, the result is often inflammation and pain.

The disease can be cured only by growing out of it — once the young person has reached the end of his or her major growth period the problem should cease. However, if a cyclist with Osgood-Schlatter's Disease continues to ride, a bone fragment may occur and require surgery. It is difficult but necessary for some enthusiastic young riders to turn to sports such as swimmming for several years.

Baker's cyst

When cyclists have a torn cartilage, arthritis or other chronic problem, fluid can accumulate behind the knee and result in swelling. Usually a

Baker's Cyst is painless, but the knee should be x-rayed to find the cause of the problem.

Kneecap dislocation

During a fall which involves a blow to the knee, the patella can be dislocated. The result is extreme pain and/or swelling, and the kneecap might actually look out of place. If you cannot push it back into position, go to an emergency room for professional attention. Use ice to reduce swelling.

Cyclists with a chronic condition where the patella slips out should undertake a program of strengthening exercises. The other option is surgery. A knee that tends to pop out at random may lead to the additional problem of chondromalacia.

Overuse injuries

Sooner or later many cyclists develop inflammation of one or more structures of the knee, causing tendinitis, bursitis, synovitis or another type of overuse injury. Again, a contributing factor is improper position. Primary culprits include rapid increases in weekly mileage without giving the body time to adjust, and riding in cold weather without good knee protection.

Tendinitis

Tendons attach muscle to bone. When a tendon in the knee is put under undue stress by improper seat or foot position or the use of large gears, it can become inflamed. Pain during movement and swelling is the result.

Once again the best treatment is rest. But if you must train or compete, it will help to use heat before and ice after. Aspirin, taken at the rate of six or eight each day, will relieve the inflammation. A doctor may prescribe one of the more common anti-inflammatory drugs, such as indocin, motrin, nalfrom or butazolidin. Should rest, aspirin and other drugs fail, you may want to turn to cortisone injection. There are risks with this, so make an informed decision only after full consultation with a physician.

Bursitis

The bursa lubricate and protect the knee and surrounding area. Bursitis can develop from a blow to the knee or arise from poor position and overuse. It is a difficult injury to self diagnose as it may produce either local or diffuse pain during cycling. It may take a physician to make the correct assessment.

Mild bursitis will respond well to rest, ice and aspirin therapy. In se-

Accidents are not the only cause of knee injuries in cyclists. Saddle height, cleat position, the weather, and foot abnormalities may also contribute.

vere cases where swelling is evident, a physician will remove the fluid with a needle. Anti-inflammatory drugs or cortisone injections may also be used.

Synovitis

Synovitis is more commonly known as water on the knee. It is an over-use injury of the synovium, which secretes lubricating fluid. Inflammation causes large quantities to be released, resulting in swelling. In severe cases the knee will have to be drained. Rest, ice and aspirin constitute the best treatment.

Ligament injuries

Mild injuries to ligaments, which attach bone to bone, can result from stretching due to overuse, improper position, or from an abnormal twisting of the knee in an accident. Usually a little pain and inflammation are the only problems, and complete recovery can be expected after a week to 10 days of rest and application of ice.

Ligament damage that is moderate (partial tear) or severe (complete rupture) usually requires immobilization of the knee in a cast for a period of three to six weeks. Surgery is almost always required to properly repair a severly injured ligament.

Torn cartilage

The major cause of cartilage problems in cyclists is an accident that gives the knee a severe twist and tears this flexible connective tissue. The rider may actually hear the knee pop and will certainly experience a brief period of acute pain. However, torn cartilage is often hard to diagnose since there may be no swelling and the knee may seem to be okay — until the next time it experiences a hard rotation. Sometimes the knee will feel as if it wants to give way, and there may be a tendency for it to click or lock, all depending on the severity of the injury.

The decision to remove torn cartilage should be made by an experienced sports orthopedic surgeon. Some mild cases will respond well to strengthening exercises.

Prevention of knee problems

The common denominator in treating cyclists' knee problems is rest or a reduction in mileage, depending on the extent of the injury. Since most ailing knees are caused by training errors or improper position on the bicycle, the following advice should be considered:

1. Avoid large gears early in the season and complete an adequate warm-up before the start of a race.

2. Always keep the knees warm, whether it be with tights or by coating with some form of lubrication.

3. Shoe cleats must be correctly positioned. It does not take too much toe-in or toe-out to stress the knee and cause an injury.

4. Proper saddle position is critical. Have this checked by an experienced cyclist or coach.

Early treatment is a must for any knee problem that shows up. Apply ice to the specific area of pain until the skin turns red, then do stretching exercises. By stretching slowly and gently you can prevent many injuries and ease those that do occur. Stretch before, after and, if necessary, during each ride.

At the first sign of a knee problem take a day or two off the bike. This may be all that's needed to avoid the road to serious injury. It makes more sense to miss a couple of rides rather than risk winding up on the shelf for several weeks.

23.
Preventing
muscle soreness

"**M**y legs feel so heavy and sore I can't lift them. I'm going to stay in bed all day."

Common words after your first race or early season ride. Everyone occasionally experiences muscle soreness eight to 48 hours after hard effort. What causes this muscle soreness that makes walking down steps or depressing the clutch pedal of the car so difficult? Why does this soreness persist for days after the race? Many cyclists erroneously believe that such a soreness comes from a buildup of lactic acid that can be mitigated by warming down after a ride. Although lactic acid is often responsible for soreness felt during and right after cycling, research has shown that next day soreness has other causes and should be handled differently.

Muscle soreness is generally classified into two types, immediate and delayed. Both types are related to cycling in excess of what you are accustomed to doing regularly. The immediate type becomes apparent during, or soon after, the ride is discontinued, and, although uncomfortable, it passes quickly and usually causes little residual loss of function. Immediate muscle soreness is probably related to a temporary energy or metabolic imbalance that is corrected by rest and readjustment of body fluids and electrolytes.

If the cycling is intense enough to produce a lack of blood flow (ischemia), the resulting build up of lactic acid and metabolic waste products causes more severe pain, which continues until the exercise intensity is reduced or stopped and the blood flow increases again.

The second type of exercise-induced muscle discomfort — delayed soreness — doesn't come or go as quickly. Instead, it appears 24 to 48 hours after strenuous riding and is usually asssociated with significant loss of muscular function and restriction of one's normal physical activities.

There are currently three theories to explain this type of soreness. One of the oldest, Hough's Torn Tissue hypothesis, is aptly named. It holds that an untrained muscle group can be damaged when subjected to a prolonged period of work. Microscopic tears occur in the muscle fibers.

Massage is an obvious remedy for the kind of muscle soreness that comes immediately after an event. But what can you do to prevent or cure the soreness that persists for days afterward?

In the early 1960s de Vries suggested that exercise promotes ischemia, which results in the production of pain substance. Once accumulated in sufficient quantities, the theory goes, this substance stimulates pain endings within the muscle. The pain, in turn, produces more reflex spasms which cause more ischemia.

The third prominent theory is based on observations that the connective tissue of the muscle is irritated or torn by exercise. The connective tissue is the fibrous material that holds the muscle cells together and attaches them to bones. Hydroxyproline, a building block of connective tissue, has been found in the urine of subjects with delayed muscle soreness. This suggests that excessive physical activity may temporarily weaken the musculo-tendon unit.

Whatever its cause, there is no medical cure for this next-day muscle soreness. Still, there are a few basic preventive measures you can take.

Gradually increase training frequency, intensity, and duration. Races or rides should not be more than twice the average daily training mileage. Avoid sudden increases in distance or speed. Stretch before and after your ride to help muscles move more easily. Use passive or non-bouncing stretching. Hold the position for approximately 60 to 90 seconds without bouncing. Then relax for one minute, and stretch again for another 60 to 90 seconds.

Mild physical activity after an exhausting race is therapeutic. It serves to maintain muscle blood flow, which will assist in releaving the swelling in the muscle. Riding slowly on the days after a hard race will help decrease the discomfort of delayed muscle soreness.

As a last resort, take two aspirin before riding and again afterwards. An anti-inflammatory agent, aspirin may help to prevent swelling that some believe is connected to soreness. Aspirin appears to be safe for most people before exercise, but be careful because it brings on sweating and can cause dehydration. Be sure to drink plenty of fluids — about eight ounces every 15 to 20 minutes during the ride. People with ulcer, kidney problems or asthma should consult their physician before trying this.

The cure to muscle soreness is prevention and proper training. If muscles are gradually trained for both endurance and strength and if stretching is a part of your total program, soreness may become a thing of the past.

24.
Does cycling protect you from heart disease?

Many serious cyclists say that one important reason they ride is to have a long and healthy life. They believe that thanks to cycling their chance of falling victim to coronary heart disease is virtually nil. They've heard reports that strongly suggest an inverse relationship between the amount of physical activity and the incidence of heart ailments.

Several "risk factors" have been cited as possible causes of heart attacks: excess weight, high blood pressure, smoking, and high levels of blood cholesterol. Cyclists score well on the first three, being lean, non-smoking, and having normal blood pressure.

But in terms of exercise's effect on cholesterol level, the evidence is controversial. It was not until the mid-'70s that awareness of a new risk factor — high-density lipoprotein — began to receive strong attention. To understand how cholesterol, fats, and lipoproteins relate to exercise and heart disease we need to review a little biochemistry and physiology.

Cholesterol

Cholesterol is an essential part of cell walls, sex hormones and bile salts. Early research found it to be a main constituent of plaques (soft lipid accumulation on the inner wall of arteries). The conclusion: Dietary cholesterol was the villain in coronary heart disease.

Triglycerides are a form of fat that is stored in the body primarily as an energy source. The problem with cholesterol and triglycerides is in their movement in the body through the bloodstream. They do not dissolve in the blood but are carried with the help of protein; they are known as the lipoproteins.

Recent findings indicate that in terms of coronary heart disease, the amount of cholesterol carried in blood by lipoproteins may be more important than total cholesterol. In fact, cholesterol is transported in the

blood by three different forms of lipoproteins. They can't be seen by the naked eye, but scientists have classified them by their density:
- — VLDL, or very low-density lipoproteins (largest and least dense)
- — LDL, or low-density lipoproteins (middle sized)
- — HDL, or high-density lipoproteins (smallest)

A VLDL is comprised mostly of triglycerides and very little cholesterol, so a high blood-triglyceride level means a high VLDL. LDL and HDL carry most of the cholesterol, so a high level of blood cholesterol can mean large amounts of LDL or HDL, or both.

Effect on health

What effect do these various lipoproteins have on the health of cyclists? Little is known about the consequences of high VLDL levels, but having a low VLDL level (with lower blood levels of triglycerides) seems to be preferred. A high LDL level has been linked with atherosclerosis (hardening of the arteries) and heart attacks.

The following startling facts about HDL concentrations were announced recently:
- — Heart attack victims have a lower than normal HDL level
- — Human babies and laboratory animals that have elevated HDL levels are resistant to heart disease
- — Women, who have higher HDL concentrations, have lower incidences of heart attacks
- — Endurance athletes (marathon runners, cross-country skiers, cyclists) have relatively high HDL levels.

Exactly what occurs in the blood stream has been hypothesized as follows. All three lipoproteins travel through the blood vessels at high speed, being jostled against the walls by various other material in the blood. Some of the LDL infiltrate the vessel walls and deposit their cholesterol, which over a period of time develops into atherosclerosis. HDL, on the other hand, is thought to absorb cholesterol constantly from the walls and return it to the liver to help produce bile (a substance that aids in absorption and digestion of fats).

Lipoprotein profiles

When you hear the term "blood cholesterol level" remember that this is the total carried by all three lipoproteins. For example, two cyclists with identical cholesterol levels of 250 milligrams may have totally different lipoprotein profiles.

Physicians have recently begun to look at the ratio of total blood cholesterol to HDL cholesterol — the lower the ratio, the less risk of coronary disease. Studies on runners and cyclists indicate that exercise may cause a beneficial increase in the HDL level.

There are a number of other factors related to athletes that may have an effect on this ratio. For example, smoking appears to be associated with a depressed HDL level, which returns to normal when smoking is stopped. Since athletes seldom smoke, it is possible that not smoking contributes to a higher HDL level.

Also, many cyclists enjoy a beer or two after a hard training ride or race. Increases in HDL are known to occur with the administration of small amounts of alcohol. A cyclist who drinks a couple of beers or a glass of wine each day may have a HDL level about 10% higher than one who does not drink at all. On the other hand, it has been shown that runners consume the same amount of alcohol on a per-thousand-calorie basis as sedentary people, making it probable that the large differences in HDL are associated with exercise, not drinking {1}.

Many nutritional factors influence the LDL level but have little effect on HDL. Once again, exercise may be the key to raising HDL levels.

What about people who are in their 30s or 40s before they begin a training program? Will their HDL value show positive change? Several studies indicate that it will {2-3}. However, the definitive answer to the effect of endurance exercise on HDL level may not be available until long-term studies are completed on a substantial number of athletes.

The position at present is that regular exercise appears to produce beneficial changes in lipoproteins. This is in addition to the role exercise plays in controlling body weight, blood pressure, the chances that a person will smoke, etc. It can be said with some certainty, then, that cycling may work as preventive medicine in the fight against coronary heart disease.

25.
How to handle colds

While exercise may help us avoid such maladies as heart disease, it can not protect us from one of the most ubiquitous diseases known to man, the common cold. In fact, when the workload is particularly heavy and reserves lag, athletes may even be more susceptible to colds than the general population. At the recent Winter Olympic Games more than 90% of the visits to physicians were for treatment of the common cold.

Colds are caused by viruses. Incapable of livng on their own, the small particles require the human body to survive. The virus invades the lining of the nose and throat. At its worst, a cold may cause muscle aches and pains, fever and headaches. Exposure to a cold can occur simply by hand contact with an infected person or a contaminated surface. People who live or work in crowded conditions are especially susceptible to colds.

Are you more likely to catch a cold when you feel chilled, as after a hard ride or race? No. There is absolutely no evidence that cold weather, dampness or changes in temperature will lead to colds. The only reason for not cycling on a cold, damp day is that it is unpleasant, not that you are more likely to catch a cold.

The onset of a cold is usually marked by dryness or burning of the nose. Later a watery nasal discharge appears. At this point we usually begin our treatment of nasal sprays, antihistamines and decongestants. Despite the relief of symptoms they offer, these drugs do nothing to the virus nor do they prevent future complications of the cold. In fact, most of the time they make you feel tired and lethargic. Vitamin C has not been shown to be any more effective in treating cold symptoms than any other product, nor does it decrease your susceptibility to the common cold.

The most effective treatment for a cold is to liquify and warm the mucus in your lungs so that it will flow more freely and carry more of the virus tissue debris and inhaled filth from your lungs to your mouth. Adequate humidity in your living and working area is also quite important in the prevention and treatment of the cold. A home humidifier can help keep the relative humidity from dropping below 35%. You can also sit for 20 minutes or so in your bathroom, with the hot shower running, or lie in a warm bath and breathe in warm, wet air. Drinking warm fluids will also help.

Cycling outdoors in winter can aggravate dry air passages because of the low humidity associated with lower temperature. Wearing a face mask and drinking fluids will alleviate these problems.

Having a cold need not curtail your training. If a cold strikes, increase your fluid intake, use a humidifier to increase available moisture, and take aspirin to relieve the aches and pains. Unless there are complications, you should be able to maintain your cycling program.

If muscle pain increases, ear infections arise, or sore throat and colored nasal discharge appears, you should see a doctor and get antibiotics to fight the secondary bacterial infections. This is a time for rest and not for training.

Fever is your body's defense mechanism against bacterial infections. It increases metabolism so that your body will produce more antibodies to kill invading germs. Fever may also be beneficial because many germs grow best at our normal temperature of 98.6°F. They do not multiply at higher temperatures. Fever is a guide which tells you that your body is fighting bacterial infection, and you're better off resting.

As soon as your temperature returns to normal, it is all right to resume your cycling program. However, you may be surprised to discover how quickly you lose your endurance. Studies on endurance athletes show that after 10 days of not exercising, they lose 10% of their endurance. The results may be more devastating after cold associated with fever. A recent study in Sweden showed that colds associated with muscle aches and pains kept athletes from regaining their full capabilities for more than three or four months. It took that long for certain chemicals necessary for energy production to return to normal levels in the muscle.

Once the worst symptoms of the cold subside, the question becomes how to recover. This has to be an individual matter, since cyclists and diseases are not standardized. Remember as long as no fever is present, it is safe to "cycle through" colds, taking care to ride within the limits of your energy and comfort to stay warm. Gentle exercise tends to break up the congestion quicker than complete rest does. But keep the pace down so as not to induce coughing.

Colds with a fever and flu require more delicate care. A period of convalesence — first complete rest, then a gradual return to a full schedule — is a must. As a rule of thumb, for each day of fever, take it easy for two days. Four days of fever and symptoms would need an additional eight days of recovery period. Avoid hard cycling or you risk a recurrence of symptoms.

26.
Traveler's diarrhea and the athlete

Traveler's diarrhea is an illness of concern to cyclists visiting other countries. It has been most extensively studied in North Americans visiting Mexico, where about 60% of travelers are affected. Known as "turista" and "Montezuma's revenge" in Mexico, traveler's diarrhea is at least as common in Europe and the Mediterranean. Athletes visiting the Soviet Union have also suffered from it. (There it is commonly known as "Trotsky's.")

Contributory causes of the disease include changes in living habits, unusual food or drink, and viral and bacterial infections. But the major cause is a bacteria known as E. coli (Escherichia coli), which stimulates the intestine to hypersecrete fluid and electrolytes.

There are several ways to help prevent traveler's diarrhea. You can peel fruits and avoid leafy vegetables, unsanitary drinking water and ice cubes that may have been prepared from unclean water. Recently some physicians have been administering an antibiotic called doxycycline (trade name, Vibramycin). Bismuth subsalicylate, Pepto-Bismol, is also used to treat and prevent traveler's diarrhea. Its greatest benefit is that it is nearly nontoxic. In a recent study, oral doses of two ounces taken several times per day reduced the incidence of diarrhea by 50%. Whether the inconvenience of such large doses is worth the 50% chance of relief is a personal decision. In any case, the compound is extremely safe and can also be used to help treat the disease once it has occurred.

If you get traveler's diarrhea, go on a liquid diet that includes fruit juices high in potassium. As symptoms subside, add bland foods such as bananas, rice, toast and eggs. Avoid dairy foods.

I have heard of physicians administering Lomotil and Imodium to athletes. Those can actually prolong the disease by keeping the bacteria in the bowels. Most importantly, they are on the list of banned substances.

Remember also that no medication for prevention or relief should be taken without a physician's advice.

Research needs to be continued to determine the minimum dose of sub-salicylate bismuth needed for protection. No one wants to use up limited luggage space with a lot of bottles. In the end the commonsense hygenic measure of avoiding unsanitary water, ice and potentially contaminated raw foods is the cornerstone of prevention of traveler's diarrhea.

27.
Don't let jet lag drag you down

It is not uncommon for competitors to fly thousands of miles to events each year, crossing many time zones. Exactly what effect this has upon health, performance, sleeping and eating is a matter of concern to the rider who has trained hard to race well.

Most plants and animals, including man, have become synchronized with the 24-hour light-and-dark cycle. This results in what is known as the circadian rhythm, from the Latin *circa dies,* meaning "about a day." Since our body rhythms are synchronized with the light/dark cycle, we sleep, work and perform more effectively at certain times of the day than at others. Body temperature steadily drops early in the morning while we're sleeping and rises into the afternoon. Blood pressure fluctuates according to a 24-hour cycle, and hormonal functions are more efficient at certain times.

When the light/dark influence is changed, the body rhythms become desynchronized and an athlete may experience problems with sleep, digestion, alertness, performance, recovery and temperament. In females, menstrual pain and dysfunction may occur.

Upsets in the body's circadian rhythm will occur after traveling quickly through several time zones, which means on coast-to-coast as well as overseas trips. Generally, "jet lag" follows this pattern:

1-2   time zones crossed: little or no effect
3-6   time zones crossed: noticeable effect
7-10   time zones crossed: considerable effect
11-15   time zones crossed: marked effect

Guidelines for travel
Follow the guidelines below to lighten the effects of extended air travel and consequent changes in circadian rhythm:

1. In the few days before the trip, avoid riding excessive miles and don't be concerned about missing a day's training during traveling. A trip through several times zones is a workout in itself. If possible, sleep as much as you can during the flight.

2. Try to change your sleeping schedule before the trip. For instance, if you will be traveling east you should go to bed earlier and get up earlier for several days. Before traveling west, you should retire later and rise later.In this way you will adapt somewhat to the time schedule at your destination.

3. Eat lightly during the trip but drink plenty of liquids like juice and water to avoid dehydration. Avoid alcohol.

4. Do mild isometric exercises and walk around the cabin during the flight to relieve stiffness and boredom and help lessen fatigue.

5. If possible, schedule your arrival for the evening hours so that you can get a good night's sleep. Light training after arrival may aid sleep.

6. During the first few days don't let the excitement of new surroundings or the sight of unknown competitors cause you to work out too hard. Take it easy or you may get worn down and increase your chances of becoming sick.

7. Before to the trip, learn about the environment you'll be entering. Prepare for the weather conditions, customs, food, transportation, etc. This may reduce some of the stress.

Avoiding medical problems

On U.S. team trips to Europe and across the country over the last few years, inevitably one or more of the riders has come down with some form of influenza or minor injury. To help avoid such risks you can do the following:

1. Assume the worst in terms of weather conditions if you are traveling to Europe. Summers there are not like those in the U.S. unless you're going to southern France or Italy.

2. If you do get sick or injured, see a doctor. Look at it this way: You have trained hard all year. Why let a simple cold develop into something worse?

3. Avoid crowds whenever possible.

4. Be careful with your diet. If you can, stay away from uncooked food and vegetables. Drink bottled water, tea or coffee instead of tap water.

5. Don't think you can "sweat out" a cold or otherwise cure it with a sauna. Saunas are excellent for adaptation to heat and for relaxation, but during sickness a sauna may put additional stress on your system.

6. If you feel sick during a race, ease up or even drop out. It does absolutely no good to punish yourself in this situation. In fact, you may do yourself further harm.

When you return to riding after an illness, don't overextend yourself and get too tired. Take the first few days to put in some easy miles and light intervals. Once you feel fine doing that, you have probably recovered. It's better to back off and wait another day if there is any doubt.

A rider who understands how to avoid the problems of extended travel will be able to compete more effectively.

28.
Avoiding air pollution

You trained for the city Time Trial Championship for six months. You felt great during the race; however, your finishing time was minutes lower than your personal worst. What happened?

What you did not realize was that the course was situated near several industries on an eight-lane highway, both of which contributed to the high level of atmospheric pollution. You were robbed of oxygen by the high levels of carbon monoxide and were irritated by the excessive amounts of ozone in the atmosphere.

If that can happen to you in your city, imagine the situation in Los Angeles, the site of the '84 Olympics. Los Angeles records some of the highest levels of pollution in the world. According to experts from California's Air Resource Board, about 2,000 tons of total organic gasses, 1,300 tons of nitrogen oxides, 400 tons of sulfur oxides, and 1,500 tons of particulates fell on the Olympic athletes *every day*.

Athletes are at special risk to airborne contaminants because of the increased rate and depth of respiration during exercise. In addition, the transition from nasal to mouth breathing bypasses the scrubbing action of the nose.

While there are many different chemicals that pollute our urban environment, carbon monoxide and ozone deserve special notice.

Ozone

Ozone, a common and typical constituent of urban environments, is the most toxic contaminant and causes the greatest decreases in athletic performance. It is a powerful oxidizing agent and can cause an increase in airway resistance, thus leading to a lower forced expiratory performance. Ozone is produced photochemically by gasses and unburned gasoline vapors. Once created, it remains in the area for a long time.

Current research on athletes confirms that heavy exercise drastically increases ozone's toxic effects. Recent work at the Human Performance Lab at University of California, Davis, found that in simulated ozone concentrations equivalent to an average-to-bad day (0.30 parts per millions) in Los Angeles, resting subjects experienced no long impairment or discomfort. But almost half the subjects engaged in heavy exercise could not complete the 60-minute tests, and all said they could not perform normally during these conditions. Many complained of wheezing, shortness of breath, headaches and nausea.

Athletes training in high ozone areas should consider training in the early morning or evening, as concentrations tend to increase rapidly after 8 a.m. to a peak early in the afternoon (about 1 p.m.) and then decrease to near background levels by 7 p.m. Remember, it is the gas which produces ozone photochemically.

No one can predict an athlete's sensitivity to ozone, but it has been shown that sensitivity diminishes with repeated exposure. This suggests an adaptive response in the lungs as cells damaged by exposure are replaced by those more resistant. At the Institute of Environmental Stress, University of California, Santa Barbara, a study measured the effects of ozone exposure in young men for two hours each day for a week and found their sensitivity was greatest on the second consecutive day of exposure. By the fifth day, they no longer responded to the ozone. In effect, they adapted, and the greater the initial sensitivity, the longer it took for the adaptation to occur.

Despite the adaptive response, cyclists would gain little by attempting to acclimate themselves to ozone pollution. Some athletes take a long time to adapt, and others never adapt at all. In addition, we don't know whether it is a healthy adaptation similar to adapting to heat or altitude.

Carbon monoxide

Carbon monoxide is another form of air pollution found in large cities. It is emitted through car exhaust, industrial waste and cigarette smoke. Its chief danger is that it squeezes oxygen out of the circulatory process. As carbon monoxide enters the blood stream via the lungs, it readily combines with the hemoglobin in the blood. Because it can combine with hemoglobin 200 times faster than oxygen does, it can cut severely into the body's oxygen supply. Even at low concentrations of 5% of the volume of air taken into the lungs, carbon monoxide has been shown to produce headaches, dizziness, confusion, and increase in body temperature.

Of interest to cyclists is a study conducted on athletic performance after exposure to auto exhaust. A team of swimmers was driven around the Los Angeles area for an hour before a meet, while the control group remained at poolside. The control group did measurably and consistently better in competition. The implications for cycling should be clear. More than one cyclist has found himself "gassed out" by cars, busses, and motor-cycles during training or racing.

Guidelines

1. If possible, avoid cycling during the peak traffic periods, 6-9 a.m. and 4-8 p.m.

2. During the winter, if you have a choice between morning and after-noon training, choose the afternoon. In the morning, wind speeds are generally light and pollutants are not as easily dispersed as they are late in the day.

3. Avoid roads with heavy truck usage.

4. Stay as far to the right of the road as possible. A few feet can make a significant difference in exposure.

Minimize the risks of air pollution when you ride. An athlete deserves only the suffering of competition — and no more.

29.
A program for winter running

For many cyclists, winter signals a time to turn to other activities, such as running, to maintain physical fitness. This might be due to snowy and icy conditions outside or simply for a psychological change. Here's some guidelines on how you can make a successful and painless transition from cycling to running.

Regardless of the amount of time spent running, each exercise session should begin with a warm-up and finish with a cool-down. A 10-minute warm-up period should include stretching and light to moderate strength exercises. This should include jogging, push-ups, and flexibility exercises.

The cool-down should allow adequate time for various body functions to readjust to normal. The length of the cool-down is dependent on the difficulty of the exercise session and on the environmental conditions. It will normally last from five to 10 minutes and include such activities as walking, slow jogging, and stretching.

The level of training intensity that can be tolerated will vary greatly depending on your fitness, general health, age and ability to perform the activity. If you are in doubt about your state of health, you should be examined by a medical doctor before attempting any vigorous program. This is very important if you are over 30.

The training heart rate

Based on recent research, an increase in heart rate equal to 75% of the difference between resting and maximal rates will produce a training effect. If you cannot have your maximal heart rate measured, an estimate can be made by subtracting your age from 220. Therefore, as you become older, your highest attainable heart rate tends to become lower, though it must be noted that some people differ from this general rule.

Calculating a training heart rate is simple. Take the difference between your maximal and resting rates, multiply it by 0.75 and add the result to the resting rate. This is called the 75% HR max. To illustrate, let's say you are a 20-year-old with a maximal heart rate of 200 beats per minute and a resting rate of 70. The difference is 130 beats, of which 75% is 98. Adding this figure to 70 beats, you get a working heart rate of 168 beats.

From my experiences with young adult cyclists, I've found that a training heart rate in the range of 150 to 170 beats per minute appears to provide adequate stimulation to the heart and circulation. For older adults, because of the decline in maximal heart rate due to aging, a rate of 130 to 140 beats is probably adequate.

To determine exercise intensity during a workout, count your pulse, using a digital wristwatch or one with a second hand. Use your fingers to locate one of the large arteries in your neck just to the side of the Adam's apple. When the pulse is felt, count the beats for six seconds and then put a zero behind the number to give you the beats per minute.

Not every day

The duration of a workout should be based on the intensity of the activity. Exertion at a 75% HR max enables you to spread a workout session over a longer period of time than if you were doing more intense exercise. To maintain fitness during the off-season, workouts should last from 30 to 60 minutes at a 75% level.

An off-season conditioning program should be conducted four to five days a week. Surprisingly, daily vigorous workouts are not necessary to maintain optimal function of the heart, lungs, and circulatory system. Working out every other day is usually sufficient when beginning a new endurance exercise program. In fact, running is so much more stressful to the musculo-skeletal system than cycling that daily, vigorous activity is often too demanding initially. You should allow enough time between workouts for your body to recover from the unaccustomed stresses.

Expect muscle soreness at first. Even if you're a national class rider, you will discover that different sets of muscles are used in different ways when running. This soreness shouldn't be so uncomfortable that you can't run. If it is, you're overdoing it and should reduce both distance and speed until the soreness subsides. Regardless of what some believe, running is not detrimental to a cyclist. Several national cycling team riders use running as part of their off-season training program. Musculo-skeletal injuries can be kept to a minimum by incorporating stretching into the program and wearing shoes specifically designed for running.

Stretching before and after every run is most beneficial, but if this is impossible, then one stretching session a day should be done. Undeniably, running tightens the leg muscles, particularly the hamstrings. Regular stretching helps develop the flexibility in muscles, ligaments and tendons necessary for unlimited running. All stretching should be static: get into the stretched position and hold it for 30 seconds or longer. Bouncing should be avoided.

The search for the perfect running shoe can be as perplexing as the search for the perfect bicycle seat. While many sport shoes are on the market, a shoe specifically designed for distance running is what you want. A quality running shoe will help prevent or relieve muscle soreness and foot/knee problems.

Personal program

The key to a successful running program is to establish your own pace, using your heart rate during exercise as the indicator of stress. The intensity of your running should be well within your limits, at approximately a 75% HR max. To regulate your exercise intensity, count your pulse rate during or immediately at the end of a run. You will then be able to modify your workout, lessening or increasing the intensity to suit your needs.

If you have trouble running continuously for 30 to 60 minutes, try mixing in some walking. Alternate runs of 100 to 200 meters with 50-meter walks. Repeat these walking/running intervals throught the workout. The walking segments are important because they represent a semi-recovery period. This way exhaustion is never reached and muscle soreness is less likely to develop.

Once you are able to run for 10 minutes or cover a mile without stopping, walking intervals can stop. When you have reached this point, you will find that running for 30 or 45 or 60 minutes becomes much easier.

Interval training can be an efficient means of maintaining fitness when workout time is limited. It differs from continuous running because the exercise is performed at 85-95% HR max. Intensity can be controlled by altering the pace of the run, the rest interval, or the number of intervals and their distance.

No matter which program you use — continuous or interval — the cardio-respiratory endurance you have gained from cycling will be maintained.

Winter warning

In January, February and March, cold weather can be a problem during any outdoor activity. Clothing worn for running should protect and insulate your skin. Its effectiveness is dependent upon the number of layers and how well they trap air. It works better to wear several light layers than to put on a T-shirt and down jacket. When there is a little wind, dress for the cold. When the breeze is blowing at 15mph or more, make sure you wear something that will keep the wind out.

Never run without a hat. The head is one part of the anatomy which loses heat rapidly in cold weather. A pullover mask can be worn on really frigid days. Mittens will make hands warmer than gloves because they merge the heat of the hand and each finger. Feet can be kept warm by adding an extra pair of socks.

By following these recommendations on frequency, intensity, duration and environment, you should be able to carry out an off-season running program to maintain the cardiovascular fitness you've gained from cycling.

30.
Chart your pursuit strategy

Leonard Nitz has won world, Olympic and/or national championship medals in almost every track racing event. It was his father who showed me the need to keep records on track cyclists in competition, and who gave me the system to do it with.

When he shared his charts and information with me in '79, Mr. Nitz wrote, "I am glad to help spread these as a means to aid future cyclists in the kilo, 3,000 and 4,000 meters. The charting technique is most helpful to beginners, who are usually helter-skelter and irregular because they have only a vague plan and change tactics during the ride. They become discouraged. Most newcomers to the 3,000 and 4,000 events never give scheduling a thought."

All cyclists, particularly on the track, can use profiling and strategy planning. Usually when two cyclists of equal physical ability meet, the rider with the best race strategy and knowledge of the other's tactics wins. Even a superior cyclist with a poor racing plan may lose to a weak one with a better plan.

Let's investigate the physiological basis of racing and look into some procedures for collecting data. The focus will be on the 4,000-meter individual and team pursuits.

Demand for oxygen

The demand for oxygen reaches near maximum soon after the pursuit starts, but oxygen delivery to the working muscles must wait until the circulatory system catches up. Thus, the rider suffers an oxygen debt that must be repaid after the event.

Several factors are important here. The faster the start and speed, the greater the oxygen debt at the beginning of the race. In the kilometer time trial, for example, effort is so great that oxygen intake cannot catch up with demand. The oxygen debt grows constantly and lactic acid reaches high levels in the blood and muscle. Either the exercise must be stopped or its intensity greatly reduced. If a cyclist starts a pursuit too fast, or tries to maintain too fast a speed, or begins the final sprint too soon, lactic acid will accumulate rapidly. The rider who exceeds his aerobic capacity may lose the race because of the early onset of fatigue.

A high maximal oxygen uptake and an effective aerobic training program are essential for the pursuiter. In sustained high-speed cycling, the payoff is more work completed before a significant oxygen debt is incurred. We also know that aerobic capacity gains importance in events lasting more than two minutes. This doesn't mean that anaerobic training should not be an integral part of the program; it is especially important in the final preparation stages.

A better way

The above problems should not occur if a pursuit is planned properly. Basically, the cyclist should try to maintain a steady pace at sufficient speed, then finish with an all-out effort.

A cyclist using this steady-state strategy will produce an early oxygen debt but keep it to a minimum. Only in the final laps does he increase speed and suffer the consequences. But with a fast finish after an economical distribution of energy during the earlier laps, he can achieve top performance.

Pacing, although wise from a physiological point of view, places great psychological stress on some pursuiters. Usually this method makes the cyclist slower than his opponent in the first few laps. This can mean trouble since a pursuiter has no control over his opponent. It is not surprising, then, that almost everyone selects a strategy designed to get out to an early lead.

Since starting at very high speed is physiologically demanding, a rider must slow down during the middle 2,000 meters or risk blowing up. He may slightly increase in the last 1,000 meters, depending on lactic acid build-up and conditioning. However, speed in the last 1,000 or 500 meters almost never increases substantially for pursuiters using this classical approach to the event (see figure 1).

Using a planned strategy, a rider will be behind during the first half of the race, then gradually close the gap by maintaining an even, sufficient speed. Then he will use his reserve of energy to move into the lead and win. You can deliver quite a psychological blow to an opponent when you start closing in as he desperately tries to keep the lead. Of course, success also requires good riding technique, good equipment, and excel-

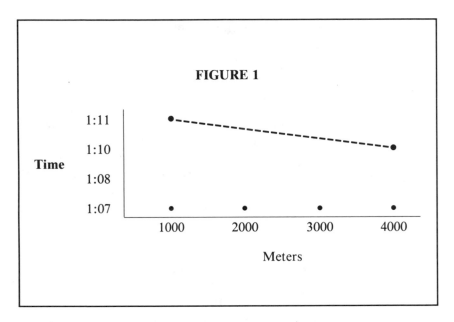

lent conditioning. Strategy can work against an opponent of comparable ability; it doesn't mean you will beat a rider who does 4:55 if your personal best is 5:05.

Twigg's example

Table 1 illustrates how well the strategy can work. The figures come from the 1982 finals of the women's 3,000-meter pursuit world championship in England.

TABLE 1

	Twigg		Carpenter	
Meters	Split	1000 M Time	Split	1000 M Time
1000	1:20:88	1:20:88	1:19:34	1:19:34
2000	2:37:20	1:16:32	2:37:03	1:17:69
3000	3:51:95	1:14:75	3:52:63	1:15:60

Pacing is a strategy which has won several world championships for U.S. pursuiter Rebecca Twigg.

Prior to the finals, Connie Carpenter was the strong favorite. But when the race ended, the gold medal was awarded to the smarter cyclist on the Leicester track that day, Rebecca Twigg.

The table shows the pursuit as it unfolded, with splits and 1,000-meter times for both cyclists. Using a slower start, Twigg was able to increase her speed steadily and ride the final 2,000 meters faster than Carpenter. In the final laps she had the energy to surge into the lead and win by several lengths.

Information about how your opponents race can help you plan a winning strategy, too. Record data at meets each season, then find the patterns. Note weather and track conditions because these can have a big effect on times. In fact, windy conditions place even more importance on the physiological aspects of a pacing strategy. The cyclist must be able to make the correct effort with and against the wind. He must know his physical capabilities perfectly.

The same profiling and strategy planning also works for road events like individual and team time trials. All riders can benefit from using this system in their racing program.

31.
Windload device tops rollers in test

Rollers are a popular substitute for outdoor riding if you live in a wintry climate or your daily schedule doesn't allow any daylight hours for training. Rollers will help you work up a good sweat, but do they provide the cardiovascular benefits of actual cycling? It is now widely recognized that they do not.

A better concept in indoor riding is available through Racer-Mate, Inc., a subsidiary of Flo Scan Instrument Co., of Seattle. This "windload simulator" is installed on your bicycle and uses forwardly curved fan blades, turned by the rear wheel, to draw air in and disperse it radially. The acceleration of air mass creates a torque on the Racer-Mate wheels that increases exponentially with speed, just like the wind on the road.

The Work Physiology Laboratory at Ohio State University conducted tests to determine if rollers or the Racer-Mate stressed cyclists substantially enough to produce a training effect. Six well trained cyclists were tested for maximal oxygen consumption and maximal heart rate on a Monarch ergometer during a progressive stress test. The measure of the maximum amount of oxygen a person can consume per minute is an excellent test for determining aerobic power. Heart rate was measured to determine cardiovascular response to the workload.

After the ergometer tests, the cyclists used their own bikes for rides on the rollers (Weyless brand) at 90rpm in gears of 52x17, 52x15 and 52x13; then they did three identical rides on the Racer-Mate. During all rides 250-gram tubular tires inflated to 90psi were used. All physiological measurements were taken with the cyclists in steady state.

The graphs show heart rate and oxygen consumption results for each of the three workloads. On the rollers the mean heart rate was 66%, 70% and 76% of maximum while pedaling in 52x17, 52x15 and 52x13, respectively. While riding at the same workload (gears) on the Racer-Mate, heart

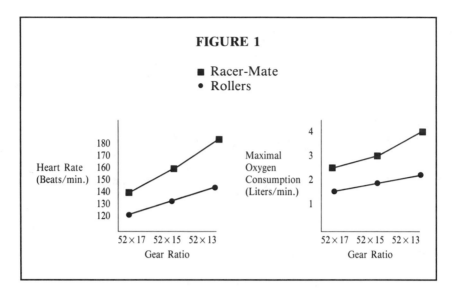

FIGURE 1

■ Racer-Mate
• Rollers

rates reached 72%, 84% and 97% of maximum. Oxygen consumption ranged from 40% to 50% while riding the rollers, compared with 48% to 85% on the Racer-Mate.

From these results it is easy to see that the Racer-Mate stresses a cyclist to a greater extent. None of the subjects could last longer than four to five minutes while riding the Racer-Mate in 52x13 at 90rpm.

When asked for their subjective judgements after riding each apparatus, every cyclist replied that the Racer-Mate stressed him more and felt more like actual on-the-road training. The only negative comments were that the Racer-Mate stand tended to flex slightly under hard pedaling.

While rollers are capable of stressing a cyclist's cardiovascular system to some extent, the Racer-Mate offers both greater resistance and the feeling of actual road training.

32.
Improve your form
with videotaping

Videotaping is an invaluable aid in sports coaching. In cycling it can revolutionize the teaching of skills, aid in the analysis of a rider's performance and discern errors that are difficult to see with the eye. It can also be fun and motivational for both coach and riders. We use videotapes as a teaching tool at the U.S. Cycling Federation camps for Juniors at the Olympic Training Center.

Two types of videotape units exist: reel-to-reel and cassette. The latter is the most popular since the tape is enclosed, thus reducing the possibility of damage in handling. A two-hour videotape cassette costs about $10-20. The tapes are reusable and inexpensive to film and they are easy and inexpensive to duplicate. Videotape recording requires less light than conventional film, and therefore recording is easier.

Early videotaping units were quite expensive, especially in comparison with the cost of movie film, but mass production and technology have now brought the price down. Today a portable videotape recorder sells for around $1,000. A black and white video camera goes for as low as $300 and a color camera for $800. A color unit brings out more detail and has much more impact.

Portable video cameras with slow motion capabilities are about $2,500 but in the near future the price should come down to about $1,500. For under $4,000 a coach can obtain a unit with slow motion, still frame, sound dubbing, portable power packs, and many other features.

Videotaping can give instant feedback during training or actual competition. Riders see their performances immediately, detect their mistakes and improve in subsequent heats or periods of the same competition.

Replaying the videotape several times is also useful, since it's easy to be distracted the first or second time and miss the finer points of the action.

You may not have access to equipment as specialized as this, but even a basic video system can provide the kind of footage that will help coaches and riders analyze and improve cycling technique.

When reviewing the material, use visual cues. Keep your detailed comments of the tape to a minimum and let the riders try to find their mistakes. "Look at the line you took into the final turn preparing for the sprint." "What position did you maintain the saddle during the steepest part of the climb?" "Observe your position after pulling off the front in the team pursuit."

A relatively experienced cyclist can recognize his mistakes, but very few can apply this information and develop specific performance adjustments to correct them. This is where a coach can help.

Recently we have begun taking a video unit to the world championships and have been scouting the other cyclists. The tape captures the opponent's strengths and weaknesses and allows the coach and rider to observe opponents before the next competition. This information is valuable in match sprints.

Videotapes can be used for instructional packages in clinics and seminars. A coach's presentation with videotape could be developed around problem-solving discussions, rather than lectures. They can also be used for promotional purposes like fund raising or publicity for your club.

As for shooting techniques, one way to ensure attention to the relevant aspects of performance is to zoom in. Be sure not to overuse the zoom feature, though. Balance details of the action with the overall view of the event. Change the angle of the camera from time to time to show different aspects of the performance. Notice how many different angles are used in the instant replays of televised sports and how much this variety adds for the viewer. However sophisticated the unit is, though, it is only as effective as its use. The imagination of the coach is the only limitation.

The advantages of using videotape are enormous. A system could be your club's biggest investment, but it will benefit your training program tremendously.

33.
A guide to cold-weather fabrics

Winter clothing should be selected for its ability to help you (1) maintain the normal core temperature of 98.6°F, and (2) dissipate the excess heat and moisture generated by cycling.

The combination of moisture, air movement and extreme cold can be devastating to a rider. Wind accelerates the loss of body heat. Moisture is an even greater danger; it conducts heat more than 30% faster than air. The greater the difference between the temperature of the body and the surrounding air, the faster the heat transfer. The longer the ride, the more effect these factors have on comfort and safety.

Insulation

Until recently, clothing insulation was thought to be exclusively a function of thickness. Now it is known that three other factors also are important: fiber reaction to moisture, heat conduction, and resistance to wind.

Fabrics with low specific gravities are good insulators. Polypropylene, for example, has a specific gravity of 0.91 and is one of the better insulating materials on the market.

The lower the thermal conductivity of a fabric, the better it will retard the flow of heat away from the body. Cotton, we'll see below, is much more heat conductive than some of the man-made materials.

Evaporative ability is the rate at which a fabric dries once it is wet. The faster it dries, the shorter the time its insulating effectiveness is reduced.

In dry conditions, it is mainly the thickness of a garment that determines its warmth. One inch of cotton can be as warm as one inch of down. The basic function of fabric as insulation is to still the air and trap heat. Its thermal conductivity is of little concern in a dry situation.

Cold, wet riding conditions and the need for extra clothing are not restricted to winter. This is the famous seven-hour Paris-Roubaix race held in Europe each April.

Any garment has some ability to trap air. How much depends on the frictional resistance of the material. On the average, fabrics trap about one-eighth inch of air. Without considering the thickness of the material itself, four layers of fabric will provide one-half inch of insulation.

However, if wind is able to penetrate the clothing, the insulation is less effective. This makes it important in high-wind situations (including long downhills) for the outermost garment to stop air penetration.

Moisture, whether from sweat, rain or snow, is a constant problem in cold-weather cycling because it reduces the ability of fabrics to insulate. In fact, water conducts heat 32 times better than air. This makes it important to understand how the various fabrics found in cycling clothing are affected by moisture.

Wool

Wool has been the choice of cyclists for years. It provides warmth, breathes, and retains body heat even when wet. It can absorb up to 16% of its own weight without feeling damp or losing its insulating ability. These advantages result from the many dead spaces that form along the surfaces of the fuzzy fibers, and their natural tendency to mat when wet.

Wool has some drawbacks, however, and in recent years has lost some popularity. It is expensive, it can shrink or lose shape, and it is relatively heavy and bulky for its insulation value. Wool also can feel too warm on mild days or during periods of hard exertion.

New processing techniques are producing wool-blend and treated-wool fabrics that won't shrink or stretch and are easy to care for. However, they usually sacrifice some degree of natural wool's best qualities, such as insulating ability.

Cotton

A characteristic of cotton that makes it excellent for summer but a hazard for winter is its high thermal conductivity (five times greater than some other fibers). Body heat, which must be retained for safe cold-weather riding, leaves through cotton and escapes into the atmosphere.

Cotton absorbs moisture well, which suggests that it would be good for removing perspiration. But wet cotton transfers heat up to 200 times faster than dry cotton, and it does not dry quickly. This makes cotton a poor choice for winter clothing.

Cotton often is blended with other fibers to enhance their softness, appearance and breathability.

Synthetics

Nylon and polyester act basically the same in the presence of water. They resist moisture and dry quickly. Nylon has several slight advantages for winter, including feeling warmer because it does not conduct heat as readily. It has a lower specific gravity, and it will absorb more water before feeling wet.

Lycra allows perspiration to pass through quickly. It also reduces the effect of wind resistance by fitting like a second layer of skin. It has little insulation ability by itself, so its place in winter cycling is in layering.

Acrylic was developed to provide the benefits of wool but at lower cost. It actually comes closer to nylon in fiber characteristics. Its insulation value comes from thickness and low density. Acrylic can wick moisture away from the skin.

Pile garments are becoming popular as a second layer. Pile is a 100% nylon or polyester fabric. It resembles cropped sheepskin but is less expensive than wool. Pile maintains its thickness when wet, thereby trapping air for maximum insulation. It dries faster than wool and is lighter for its equivalent mass. Since pile will not stop wind and water, an outer shell is necessary.

Gore-Tex

There are other new fabrics which mean good news for cyclists who train year round. W. L. Gore & Associates have been manufacturing microporous polytetrafluorethylene (PTFE) membranes for the scientific and medical communities for years. Artificial arteries and heart patches, for example, use PTFE membranes. More commonly known under the Dupont tradename of Teflon, the PTFE membrane has nine billion tiny pores per square inch. Each pore is 700 times larger than a water vapor molecule, but thousands of times smaller than a drop of liquid water. The membrane is remarkably lightweight, weighing only one-half ounce per square yard.

The PTFE membrane can be bonded to any durable material for use in an almost unlimited variety of products — from shoes to gloves to outerwear. In the mid '60s Gore began laminating their membrane to rainwear fabric. Gore-Tex fabric is composed of a microporous membrane protected on one or both sides by fabric.

Gore-Tex offers waterproof protection because of the hydrophobicity (water-hating quality) of PTFE and because of the microporous nature of the membrane. Waterproof fabric is specified by the U.S. military as fabric which will not admit water at pressures of 25psi. Gore-Tex fabric will withstand more than 110psi before water penetrates. In comparison, 60/40 cloth and 1.8 oz nylon taffeta materials are rated at 0psi.

Since the membrane's pores are so small and also misaligned, the fabric is windproof. The dead air barrier reduces convective heat loss, keeping you much warmer than conventional fabric.

Gore-Tex fabric is also highly breathable. Breathability is measured in terms of the transmission of moisture vapor through a fabric over a specified period of time. Since the pores of the membrane are so much larger than an individual molecule of water vapor, perspiration vapor diffuses through the fabric. This allows a higher degree of comfort than ever available before in waterproof fabric.

While there were some problems with the first generation of Gore-Tex (e.g., contamination from body oils) a second generation Gore-Tex was introduced in 1978. There are few problems today, very few delaminations, and better waterproofing and breathability, if you wash the fabric properly and drip or tumble dry at a low setting.

There are sometimes complaints about Gore-Tex not working as well as the literature states. Much of this has to do with the concentration of water vapor. The vapor flows towards the side of the membrane that has the least concentration of moisture (humidity). Another point to remember is that Gore-Tex slows down the transfer of the vapor from one side to the other. This is why, on days of high humidity when you are exercising heavily, Gore-Tex will not be as effective.

To get the most from your Gore-Tex clothing, wear a minimum of other clothing under your Gore-Tex garment. This will prevent you from overheating and oversweating which produces excess water vapor.

Use convection currents to your advantage by ventilating as much as possible. These currents will remove excess vapor, as well as keep the body from overheating. The general rule is: Wear Gore-Tex as close to your body as possible, closing down sleeves, zippers, hoods, etc., just enough to prevent the rain and wind from entering.

Polypropylene

The days of the wool jersey and the sweat shirt may be numbered. Polypropylene, a new fiber, offers lighter weight, greater breathability and better insulation. Polypropylene is now used for everything from jerseys, pullovers and jackets to leg liners.

Polypropylene is also known for its hydrophobic quality. Instead of absorbing moisture as cotton does, it wicks moisture away from your body, keeping you dry and comfortable while you're cycling and sweating heavily.

Its wickability makes polypropylene the garment to wear next to your skin. In addition it is lightweight, insulating, highly abrasion resistant and quick drying — all good news to cyclists who must wash their garments several times a week.

Some athletes wear a light layer of polypropylene close to the skin and cover that with a second layer of heavier weight polypropylene. This way they get insulation without weight, and take full advantage of the material's wicking factor. Follow this up with a Gore-Tex suit and you have the perfect cold weather clothing system.

Polypropylene garments do require some special care. Washing by hand will reduce the amount of pilling that occurs. Polypropylene will melt if put into hot water or in a dryer, but since it air dries very quickly, it should not need machine drying anyway.

34.
Choose light colors for summer jerseys

When sponsors order clothing for their teams, they should do it with an eye towards protecting riders from the hot summer sun. The color and type of fabric are the two main considerations.

In general, light colors feel cooler than dark colors when worn in sunlight. White is the coolest of all. Yet each season there are team jerseys featuring dark colors. There are practical advantages to dark colors, such as covering ability (the same thin, porous fabric in a light color may let the skin show through) and the tendency of dark colors to hide dirt and stains.

But the fact remains that a black suit will absorb up to 95% of the energy of sunlight, while a white suit may absorb as little as 30%. The value for an intermediate hue is 50%.

A fabric's texture is as important as its color. A loosely woven material is better than a tight weave; it will let the air through to help evaporate moisture and cool the body. The new materials, such as Lycra, are excellent because they are light and they stretch for a comfortable fit. In addition, moisture passes through them quickly and they won't become heavy with rain or sweat.

Clothing companies would do well to incorporate the mesh materials now used in running singlets. Mesh panels in the sides and lower front of jerseys would expose more skin surface to the cooling air. White panels on the sides and front of shorts might help in long road races.

Proper clothing for hot-weather riding gets complicated when all factors are considered. Temperature, wind, solar radiation and terrain all are important. Furthermore, riders are affected differently by the conditions. Plenty of variation is possible, but black should by no means be the primary color for a summer jersey.

35.
Some books for
your sports library

With the help of the Sports Medicine Library at the Olympic Training Center, I compiled a list of resource books which can be useful to the cyclist. Here are four on sportsmedicine and psychology. The annotations are mine.

The Female Athlete: A Coach's Guide to Conditioning and Training. By Carl Klafs and M.J. Lyon. St. Louis: C.V. Mosby, 1978. $11.95.

This book presents facts on the anatomical and physiological differences between women and men discusses and the effects of a woman's physical characteristics on her performance. The female is considered in terms of her body type, cardiovascular and respiratory system, injury incidence, nutritional needs, heat adaptation, body composition, gynecological factors such as pregnancy and the postpartum period, secondary amenorrhea, and response to the stress of sports.

The book is directed to coaches with little science background, and it will also serve as an excellent source for the female competitor. Each chapter contains references and a suggested reading list. The authors bring under one cover the many issues that pertain to the female cyclist's needs.

Anabolic Steroids and Sports. By James Wright. Natick, MA: Sports Science Consultants, 1978. $9.95.

The role of anabolic steroids in both amateur and professional cycling is an increasingly controversial issue. This book deals directly with the hazards and benefits derived from the use of the substances.

Chapters on sports-related drug use, the role of hormones in cell growth, the relative safety and effectiveness of steroids, and a summary of 25 human studies give the reader an overview of this important topic.

Research results lead to the conclusion that the major physiological threat comes not from using the drugs with appropriate guidance, but from taking larger and larger quantities (up to 50 times the recommended dose) over a long period of time. This is apparently common practice among serious athletes. Unfortunately, the long-term effects of the drugs are not yet known.

Directed primarily to athletes, coaches and trainers, this book is an excellent review of the literature dealing with anabolic steroids. It is currently available only by mail order from Sports Science Consultants, 11 Heritage Lane, Natick, MA 01760.

Medicine for Sport. By David Apple and John Cantwell. Chicago: Year Book Medical Publishers, 1979, $19.95.

This is a highly readable, concise yet thorough book for those involved in treating cyclists or for the cyclist themselves. It includes a practical view of exercise physiology and nutrition. It discusses current medical and cardiac concepts as they pertain to athletes.

Both authors are physicians with backgrounds in treating athletes. They call upon their expertise in general medicine, cardiology and orthopedics to give a timely reference which covers such topics as fuel consumption, muscle type and function, carbohydrate loading, the athlete's heart, different types of exercise and benefits, and more. Numerous charts and tables accompany the text.

Sports Psychology: An Analysis of Athletic Behavior. William Straub. Ithaca: Movement Press.

Some of the foremost authorities in the field have contributed articles to this book, which is designed to communicate all the important principles of sport psychology to the coach or cyclist. Anyone who wants to know more about meditation and performance, personality of the athlete, aggressions, leadership, and team cohesion should read this work.

Dr. Straub has assembled a book on sport psychology that is well-founded and accurate. It is highly recommended to anyone with an interest in sport.

Books on nutrition

The following list focuses on nutritional books in the athletic arena, even though they are not specifically written for the cyclist. They will provide information for the athlete, coach and trainer who wants to learn more about nutrition and athletic performance. With some exceptions, these books provide sound information in an understandable way.

American Association of Health, Physical Education and Recreation and Dance. *Nutrition for Athletes. A Handbook for Coaches.* Washington, DC: AAHPERD, c.1971 (1980 printing). 63 pp. $5.95.

Here's a concise source of nutrition information written for coaches and athletic directors. The basic diet and current theories of nutrition and athletics are analyzed. Special problems of pre-competition food intake and dietary supplements are discussed and evaluated.

Astrand, P. O. *Health and Fitness*. New York: Barron's/Woodbury, 1977. $3.95.

Dr. Astrand describes the benefits of exercise in terms of health, fitness and weight maintenance. He offers many suggestions for physical conditioning programs.

Bogert, L. J., G.M. Briggs and D.H. Calloway. *Nutrition and Physical Fitness,* 9th ed. Philadelphia: W. B. Saunders Co., 1973. 598 pp. (out of print).

Basic facts of nutrition with emphasis on building strong bodies and maintaining a high degree of health and vigor. Authors go beyond the general text and relate principles of nutrition to physical fitness and well-being.

Buxbaum, Robert, M.D. and Lyle J. Michelli, M.D. *Sports for Life: Fitness, Training, Injury Prevention and Nutrition*. 1979. 204 pp.

Clark, Nancy. *The Athlete's Kitchen*. Boston: CBI Publishing, 1981. 322 pp. $9.95.

Discusses the nutrition and human performance link and gives recipes for athletes who want to have the competitive edge.

Costill, David L. *A Scientific Approach to Distance Running*. Los Altos, CA: Track & Field News, 1979. 128 pp. $5.00.

A digest of the technical aspects of research that form the scientific basis for old and new concepts about distance running.

Darden, Ellington. *Nutrition and Athletic Performance*. Alhambra, CA: Borden Press, 1976. 208 pp. $7.95.

Information for athletes, coaches and trainers who want to learn more about nutrition and athletic performance.

Darden, Ellington. *Nutrition for Athletics*. North Palm Beach, FL: Athletic Institute, 1975. $7.95.

Darden, Ellington. *Olympic Athletes Ask Questions about Exercise and Nutrition*. Anna-Pub. $2.95

Darden, Ellington. *The Superfitness Handbook*. Philadelphia: George F. Stickley Co., 1980. 296 pp. $12.95.

Includes proper care for injuries along with guidelines for treatment, rehabilitation, and prevention of the most common complaints. Discusses heart-lung endurance and proper nutrition for keeping fat off.

Eisenman, Patricia. *Coaches' Guide to Nutrition and Weight Control*. Champaign, IL: Human Kinetics, 1982. 255 pp. $9.95.

Food for Fitness. Mountain View, CA: World Publications, 1975. 143 pp. $6.75.

Galandek, Diana J. *Food for Fitness: The Physical Education Teacher's Handbook*. New Orleans: St. Mary's Dominican College, 1981. 171 pp.

Getchell, Bud. *Physical Fitness: A Way of Life*, 2d ed. New York: John Wiley and Sons, 1979. 352 pp.

Provides sound information for developing a systematic program of exercise and physical activity that best fits the individual needs. The relationship between nutrition, weight control, heart disease and exercise are explored.

Getchell, Bud. *Being Fit: A Personal Guide*. New York: John Wiley and Sons, 1982. 312 pp.

Haskell, William. *Nutrition and Athletic Performance*. Palo Alto, CA: Bull Publishing Co., 1982. 284 pp. $19.95.

Katch, F. I. and W. D. McArdle. *Nutrition, Weight Control and Exercise*. Boston: Houghton Mifflin, 1977. 365 pp. $15.95.

A combination of theoretical and practical information on nutrition and physiology as they pertain to exercise and weight control. Good resource for information on cardio-respiratory fitness and evaluation of body composition.

Katch, F. I., W. D. McArdle and B. R. Boylan. *Getting in Shape — An Optimum Approach to Fitness and Weight Control*. Boston: Houghton Mifflin Co., 1979. 193 pp. (out of print).

The authors show how to evaluate fitness and desirable weight and how to set up an individualized fitness and diet program. Of particular interest in the book is a researched method of finding out the proportion of fat and lean by using a tape measure and scale. The book tells how to find the right exercises and develop the incentive to keep doing them.

Lincoln, A. *Food for Athletes*. Chicago: Contemporary Books, 1979. 292 pp. (out of print)

Includes basic information about nutrients and energy requirements. Discusses problems in an athlete's performance that may be related to diet and notes nutrition requirements for particular sports.

Mann, George V. *The Care and Feeding of Athletes*. New York: Le Jacq, 1980. 124 pp. $26.00.

Milkereit, J. and H. Higdon. *Runner's Cookbook*. Mountain View, CA: World Publications, 1979, 324 pp. $16.95.

This enjoyable cookbook offers many valuable tips for the runner/athlete to use in preparing well balanced meals with a wide variety of lightly processed foods.

Morella, Joseph J. *Nutrition and the Athlete*. Van Nostrand Reinhold, 1981. $7.95. National Dairy Council.

Nutrition, Athletics and Physical Fitness. Rosemont, IL: National Dairy Council, 1978.

Paish, Wilfred H. C. *Diet in Sport*. New York: Sterling Publishing Co., 1979. 96 pp. $5.95.

Runner's World Editors. *The Complete Diet Guide for Runners and Other Athletes*. Mountain View; Anderson-World, 1978. 232 pp. $4.95.

A compilation of nutrition knowledge in the field of athletics, written for the physically active public. Topics include "Vegetarian Diets," "Athlete's Protein Needs," "Vitamins and Minerals," "Fast Doesn't Equal Faster" and "Work Off the Pounds."

Smith, N. J. *Food for Sport*. Palo Alto, CA: Bull Publishing Co., 1976. 188 pp. Paperback. $6.95.

Simple, easy-to-read language about how food affects athletic performance . Appropriate for coaches or athletes as well as those health professionals involved in athletics.

Smith, N., et al. *Handbook for the Young Athlete*. Palo Alto, CA: Bull Publishing Co., 1978. 201 pp. $6.95.

Answers questions asked by young athletes about nutrition, injuries, athletic potential, training, women athletes and recruiting.

Williams, M. H. *Nutritional Aspects of Human Physical and Athletic Performance*. Springfield, IL: Charles C. Thomas, 1976. 456 pp. $22.50.

Review of related literature and research on nutrition for athletics and physical fitness. While not intended to be a nutrition book per se, it includes basic information about the functions and sources of specific nutrients.

36.
A list of
sportsmedicine centers

In the past several years numerous sportsmedicine centers have been established to meet the needs of the recreational athlete and the serious amateur who doesn't have the benefit of a team trainer. One of the facilities listed below may be a good place to start if you are away from home and need medical attention for a problem related to cycling. Consult your personal physician to see if he or she has any knowledge of the center you expect to visit. This is not a complete tabulation of sportsmedicine clinics, and inclusion in this list does not represent an endorsement of a center by me or *Velo-news*.

ALABAMA
U.S. Sports Academy
University of South Alabama
307 University Blvd.
Mobile, AL 36688

University Hospital Heart Station
University of Alabama
Birmingham, AL 35294

ARIZONA
Sports Medicine Clinic
Bell Road Medical Center
3010 East Bell Rd.
Phoenix, AZ 85032

Rehabilitation Medicine Sports Clinic
1500 North Wilmot, Suite 140
Tucson, AZ 85712

ARKANSAS
Preventive Health and Cardiac Rehabilitation Program
Box 2507-University of Arkansas
Monticello, AR 71655

CALIFORNIA
Orthopedic Hospital Sports Medicine Clinic
2400 South Flower
Los Angeles, CA 90007

Sports Injury Rehabilitation and Research Clinic
3340 Kemper St.
San Diego, CA 92110

Center for Sports Medicine
St. Francis Memorial Hospital
1900 Hyde St.
San Francisco, CA 94109

National Athletic Health Institute
575 East Hardy St.
Inglewood, CA 90301

Sports Conditioning & Rehabilitation
871 South Tustin
Orange, CA 92666

Dept. of Sports Medicine
Palo Alto Medical Clinic
300 Homer Ave.
Palo Alto, CA 94301

Napa Valley Physical Therapy and Sportsmedicine Center
1103 Trancas St.
Napa, CA 94558

North Tahoe Orthopedic Group
Donner Medical Center
Truckee, CA 95734

Orthopedic & Sports Physical Therapy
10631 Bandley Dr.
Cupertino, CA 95014

COLORADO
Aspen Health Center
25 Meadows Rd.
Aspen, CO 81611

Sports Conditioning & Orthopedic Rehabilitation Clinic
1919 Federal Blvd.
Denver, CO 80204

Steamboat Springs Sports Medicine, Rehabilitation, & Physical Therapy
Box 5428
Steamboat Springs, CO 80499

Fort Collins Sports Medicine Clinic
1148 East Elizabeth
Fort Collins, CO 80524

Denver Sports Medicine Clinic
2005 Franklin, 550
Denver, CO 80205

CONNECTICUT
Life Sciences Temple Medical Center
60 Temple St.
New Haven, CT 06510

Fitness & Sports Conditioning Center
20 Dayton Ave.
Greenwich, CT 06830

DELAWARE
Delaware All-Sports Research
25 Milltown Rd.
Wilmington, DE 19808

DISTRICT OF COLUMBIA
Runners Clinic, Smith Center
George Washington University
22 and G St., NW
Washington, DC 20052

Sports Medicine Clinic
Georgetown University
3800 Reservoir Rd., NW
Washington, DC 20007

FLORIDA
Life Clinic
407 Beverly Blvd.
Brandon, FL 33511

Spectrum Sport
1623 Medical Dr., Suite D
Tallahassee, FL 32308

GEORGIA
Atlanta Sports Medicine Clinic
4600 Memorial Dr.
Decatur, GA 30032

Sports Medicine Education Institute
20 Linden Ave., NE, Suite 400
Atlanta, GA 30308

Sports Medicine Clinic
615 Peachtree St., N
Atlanta, GA 30308

HAWAII
Honolulu Medical Group
Sports Medicine Dept.
550 South Beretania St
Honolulu, HI 96813

IDAHO
Idaho Sports Medicine Institute
125 East Idaho, Suite 204
Boise, ID 83702

ILLINOIS
Northwestern University Medical School
Sports Medicine Clinic
303 East Chicago Ave.
Chicago, IL 60610

Great Plains Sports Medicine Foundation
624 NE Glenn Oak Ave.
Peoria, IL 61603

Physical Therapy Services
6858 Archer Ave., South
Chicago, IL 60638

Center for Athletic Injury Research
25 Lakeside Lane
Mahomet, IL 61853

INDIANA
Indianapolis Physical Therapy & Sports Medicine
6340 West 37 St.
Indianapolis, IN 46224

Aerobics Performance Center
8158 Zionsville Rd.
Indianapolis, IN 46268

KANSAS
University of Kansas Fitness Clinic
108 Robinson Center
University of Kansas
Lawrence, KS 66045

Sports Rehabilitation Assoc.
4510 West 89 St.
Prairie Village, KS 66207

KENTUCKY
Good Samaritan Hospital
Dept. of Physical Therapy
310 South Limestone
Lexington, KY 40508

LOUISIANA
Lee Circle YMCA
936 St. Charles Ave.
New Orleans, LA 70130

MARYLAND
Sports Medicine Center
5454 Wisconsin Ave., #1555
Chevy Chase, MD 20015

Union Memorial Sports Medicine Center
201 East University Pkwy.
Baltimore, MD 21218

MASSACHUSETTS
Berkshire Sports Medicine Center
510 North St.
Pittsfield, MA 01201

Sports Medicine Resource
830 Boylston St.
Brookline, MA 02167

Sports Medicine Clinic
Massachusetts General Hospital
Fruit Street
Boston, MA 02114

Sports Medicine Clinic
250 Pond St.
Braintree, MA 02184

MICHIGAN
Sports Medicine Clinic
30730 Ford Rd.
Garden City, MI 48135

Physical Therapy & Sports Medicine
20002 Farmington Rd.
Levonia, MI 48152

MINNESOTA
St. Croix Orthopedics
13961 North 60 St.
Stillwater, MN 55082

Institute of Athletic Medicine
606 24th Ave., South, fi708
Minneapolis, MN 55454

Orthopedic Physical Therapy Service
733 Central Medical Building
St. Paul, MN 55104

MISSOURI
St. Louis Sports Medicine Clinic
14377 Woodlake Dr., Suite 311
Chesterfield, M0 63017

Metropolitan Orthopedics
522 N. New Ballas Rd., Room 199
Creve Coeur, MO 63141

MONTANA
Human Performance Laboratory
University of Montana
Missoula, MT 59812

NEW HAMPSHIRE
Catholic Medical Center
100 McGregor St.
Manchester, NH 0310

NEW JERSEY
Sports Clinic
United Hospitals Orthopedic Center
89 Park Ave.
Newark, NJ 07104

Morristown Memorial Hospital
Sports Medicine Clinic
95 Mt. Kemble Ave.
Morristown, NJ 07960

Sports Medicine Institute
Christ Hospital
176 Palisade Ave.
Jersey City, NJ 07306

Sports Medicine Center
Route 73 South
Winslow Professional Bldg.
Tansboro, NJ 08009

NEW YORK
Institute of Sports Medicine & Athletic Trauma
130 East 77 St., Room 810
New York, NY 10021

Rainbow Sports Medicine Center
566 Broadway
Massapequa, NY 11758

Dept. of Rehabilitation Medicine
Reconditioning Lab
Methodist Hospital
506 Sixth St.
Brooklyn, NY 11215

Athletic Injury Treatment Center
University of Rochester Medical Center
601 Elmwood Ave.
Rochester, NY 14642

OHIO
Rainbow Sports Medicine Center
2074 Abington Rd.
Cleveland, OH 44106

University of Cincinnati
Sports Medicine Institute
234 Goodman Ave.
Administration Bldg.
Cincinnati, OH 45267

Cleveland Clinic
9500 Euclid Ave.
Cleveland, OH 44106

Tricounty Orthopedics Surgeons Sports Medicine Clinic
3244 Bailey St., NW
Massilon, OH 44646

OKLAHOMA
Division of Sports Medicine
Oklahoma Univ. Health Sciences Center
Oklahoma City, OK 73190

OREGON
Center for Sports Medicine
132 East Broadway, Suite 830
Eugene, OR 97401

PENNSYLVANIA
Pittsburgh Physical Therapy Assoc.
11910 Perry Hwy.
Wexford, PA 19104

Sports Medicine Center
Braddock General Hospital
400 Holland Ave.
Braddock, PA 15104

Meadville Sports Medical Advisory Group
766 Liberty St.
Meadville, PA 16335

Sports Medicine Clinic
Community General Osteopathic Hospital
Box 3000
4300 Londonderry Rd.
Harrisburg, PA 17105

Pennsylvania State Sports Medicine Center
Milton S. Hershey Medical Center
Hershey, PA 17033

University of Pennsylvania
Sports Medicine Center
Weightmann Hall E-7
235 South 33 St.
Philadelphia, PA 19104

RHODE ISLAND
Institute of Preventive Medicine & Physical Fitness
100 Highland Ave.
Providence, RI 02906

TEXAS
Sports Medicine Clinic of Dallas
12140 Webb Chapel Rd.
Dallas, TX 75234

Sports Medicine & Rehabilitation Clinic
4330 Medical Dr.
San Antonio, TX 78229

Sports Medicine Clinic
9262 Forest Lane
Dallas, TX 75238

UTAH
Sportsmall Rehabilitation Center
5445 South 900 East
Salt Lake City, UT 84117

Physical Therapy & Sports Medicine
3755 Washington Blvd.
Ogden, UT 84403

VIRGINIA
Center for Sports Medicine
National Orthopedic and Rehabilitation Hospital
2455 Army Navy Dr.
Arlington, VA 22206

Peninsula/Tidewater Sports Medicine Center
2013 Cunningham Dr., Suite 310
Hampton, VA 23666

WASHINGTON
Sports Medicine Clinic
1551 NW 54 St.
Seattle, WA 98107

Spokane Sportsmedicine & Physical Therapy
West 105 Eighth
South Center Medical Bldg., #560
Spokane, WA 99203

University of Washington
Division of Sports Medicine
242 Edmunds Pavilion
Seattle, WA 98195

WEST VIRGINIA
Sports Medicine Center
Wheeling Hospital Medical Park
Wheeling, WV 26003

WISCONSIN
Sports Medicine Section
University of Wisconsin
Div. of Orthopedic Surgery
1300 University Ave.
Madison, WI 53706

Mount Sinai Sports Medicine Clinic
950 North 12 St.
Milwaukee, WI 53201

WYOMING
Teton Village Clinic for Sports Medicine & Family Care
Box 606
Teton Village, WY 83025

References

Chapter 3

1. Wilmore, Jack. Oxygen. In *Ergogenic Aids and Muscular Performance*, ed. Morgan, W. P. New York: Academic Press, 1972.
2. Karpovich, P. The effect of oxygen inhalation on swimming performance. *Research Quarterly* 5 (1934):24.
3. Ebel, E., et al. Some effects of breathing oxygen before and after exercise. *Journal of Applied Physiology* 16 (1961):48-52.
4. Miller, A. Influence of oxygen administration on the cardiovascular function during exercise and recovery. *Journal of Applied Physiology* 5 (1952):165-168.

Chapter 5

1. Suinn, Richard. Easing athletes' anxiety at Winter Olympics. *The Physician and Sportsmedicine* (March 1977).
2. Suinn, Richard. Psychology and sports performance: principles and applications. In *Sports Psychology: An Analysis of Athletic Behavior*, ed. William F. Straub. Ithaca, NY: Movement Publications, 1978.
3. Suinn, Richard. Psychological rules for competition, unpublished manuscript.
4. Suinn, Richard. Psychological preparation of U.S. Winter Olympic Team. *Psychology Today* (July 1977).

Chapter 6

1. Dyer, K. F. The trend of male-female performance differential in athletics, swimming and cycling 1948-1976. *Journal of Biosocial Science* 9 (1977):325-338.
2. Burke, Ed. Physiological characteristics of national and international competitive cyclists. *The Physician and Sportsmedicine*. In press.
3. Wilmore, Jack. The Female Athlete. *The Journal of School Health* (April 1977).
4. Costill, D. L. et al. Lipid metabolism in skeletal muscle of endurance

trained males and females. *Journal of Applied Physiology* 47 (1979):787-791.

5. Wilmore, Jack. Research studies on the female athlete: body composition and strength development. *Journal of Health, Physical Education, and Recreation* 46 (1975):38-40.

6. Hermensen, L. Oxygen transport during exercise in human subjects. *Acta Physiologica Scandinavia Supplement* (1973):399.

Chapter 9

1. Burke, Ed., Fr. Cerney, D. Costill, and W. Fink. Characteristics of skeletal muscle in competitive cyclists. *Medicine and Science in Sports* 9 (1977):109-112.

2. Issekutz, B. Jr., P. Paul, and K. Rodhal. Aerobic work capacity and plasma FFA turnover. *Journal of Applied Physiology* 20 (1965):293-296.

3. Issekutz, B. Jr., W. A. Shaw and T. B. Issekutz. Effect of lactate on FFA and glycerol turnover in resting and exercising dogs. *Journal of Applied Physiology* 39 (1975):349-353.

4. Stromme, L. B., F. Inger and H. D. Meen. Assessment of maximal aerobic capacity in specifically trained athletes. *Journal of Applied Physiology* 42 (1977):833-837.

Chapter 10

1. Burke, Ed., Fleck, S., Dickson, T. Post competition blood lactate concentrations in competitive track cyclists. *British Journal of Sports Medicine* 15, 4 (1981):242-245.

2. Kindermann, W.; Keul, J. Lactate acidosis with different forms of sports activities. *Canadian Journal of Applied Sport Science* 2 (1972): 177-182.

3. Kyle, C. R.; Mastropaolo, J. Reduction of wind resitance and power output of racing bicyclists and runners traveling in a group. *Medicine and Science in Sports* 8 (1976):56-57.

Chapter 12

1. deWijin, J. F., et al. Hemoglobin, packed cell volume, serum iron and iron binding capacity of selected athletes during training. *Nutrition and Metabolism* 13 (1971):129.

2. Stewart, G. A., et al. Observations on the hematology and iron protein intake of Australian athletes. *Medical Journal of Australia* 2 (1972):1338.

3. Clement, D. B., et al. Hemoglobin values: Comparative survey of the 1976 Canadian Olympic Team. *Canadian Medical Association Journal* 177 (1977):614.

4. Martin, R. P., et al. Blood chemistry and lipid profiles of elite distance runners. *Annals of New York Academy of Sciences* 301 (1977):346.
5. Brotherhood, J., et al. Hematological status of middle and long distance runners. *Clinical Science and Molecular Medicine* 48 (1975):139.
6. Bunch, T. V. Blood test abnormalities in runners. *Mayo Clinic Proceedings* 55 (1980):113.
7. Shiraki, K., et al. Anemia during physical training and performance. In XXth World Congress of Sports Medicine. *Congress Proceedings* Melbourne, 1974.
8. Committee on dietary allowances food and nutrition board, National Research Council. *Recommended Dietary Allowances*, 9th ed. Washington: National Academy of Sciences, 1980.
9. Bieger, W. P., et al. Exercise-induced monocytosis and modulation of monocyte function. *International Journal of Sports Medicine* 1 (1980):30.
10. Hedfors, E., et al. Variations of blood lymphocytes during work studied by cell surface markers, DNA synthesis and cytotoxicity. *Clinical Experimental Immunology* 24 (1976):328.
11. Moorthy, A. V., and Zimmerman, S.W. Human leukocyte responses to an endurance race. *European Journal of Applied Physiology* 38 (1978):271.
12. Rushall, B. S., and Rush, J. D. Hematological responses to training elite swimmers. *Canadian Journal of Applied Sport Sciences* 5 (1980):164.

Chapter 17

1. Bolin, T. D., and A. E. Davis. Primary lactase deficiency: genetic or acquired? *Digestive Diseases* 15 (1970):679-692.
2. Birch, G. G. Lactose: one of nature's paradoxes. *Journal of Milk and Food Technology*. 35 (1972):32-34.
3. Van Huss, W., et al. Effect of milk consumption on endurance performance. *Research Quarterly* 33 (1962):120-128.
4. Nelson, D. Idiosyncrasies in training and diet. *Scholastic Coach* 30 (1961):33-34.
5. Darden, E. *Nutrition and Athletic Performance*. Pasadena:Athletic Press, 1976.

Chapter 18

1. Wright, J. *Anabolic Steroids and Sports*. Natick, MA: Sports Science Consultants 1978.
2. MacDougall, D. Anabolic Steroids. *Physician and Sportsmedicine* 11, 9 (1983):95-99.

3. Taylor, W. *Anabolic Steroids and the Athlete.* Jefferson, NC: McFarland & Company 1982.
4. Johnson, F. C. The association of oral androgenic anabolic steroids and life-threatening disease. *Medicine Science and Sports* 7 (Winter 1975):284-286.

Chapter 19
1. McCrady, P. *The Persecuted Drug: The Story of DMSO.* New York:Chapter Inc., 1979.
2. Merken, G. The DMSO controversy. *The Runner* (April 1981):17.
3. Reed, J. D. A miracle? Or is it a mirage. *Sports Illustrated* (April 1981).
4. Wischnia, B. DMSO. *Runner's World* (November 1980):62-66.
5. DMSO: No proof of miracles. *F.D.A. Consumer* (September 1980):28-29.

Chapter 24
1. Wood, P. D. Running away from heart disease. *Runner's World* (June 1979).
2. Ballantyne, D., et al. The effect of physical training on plasma lipids and lipoproteins. *Clinical Cardiology* 4 (1980):1-4.
3. Leon, A. S., et al. Effects of a vigorous walking program on body composition, and carbohydrate and lipid metabolism of obese young men. *American Journal of Clinical Nutrition* 32 (1979):1776-1787.
4. Castelli, W. P., et al. HDL cholesterol and other lipids in coronary heart disease. The cooperative lipoprotein phenotyping study. *Circulation* 55 (1977):767-772.
5. Gordon, T., et al. High-density lipoproteins as a protective factor against coronary heart disease. The Framingham study. *American Journal of Medicine* 62 (1977):707-714.
6. Gaston, E. A. Bicycling, cholesterol and your heart. *Bicycling* (March 1980).

Chapter 27
1. Antal, L. C. The effect of the changes of circadian rhythm on the sport shooter. *British Journal of Sports Medicine* 9,1 (1975):9-12.
2. Caldwell, John. *Caldwell on Competitive Cross-Country Skiing.* Brattleboro, VT: Stephen Greene, 1979, 116-121.
3. LaDow, J. Circadian rhythms and athletic performance. *The Physician and Sportsmedicine* 7,7 (1979):87-93.
4. Rodahl, A., et al. Diurnal variation in performance of competitive swimming. *Swimming Technique* 13,3 (1976):93-95.

Chapter 29
1. Burke, Ed. Beware of wind-chill during early season rides. *Velo-News* (Jan. 13, 1978).
2. Daniels, J., K. Fitts and G. Sheehan. *Conditioning for Long Distance Runners.* New York: John Wiley and Sons, 1978.
3. Getchell, B. *Physical Fitness: A Way of Life.* New York: John Wiley and Sons, 1976.
4. Pollock, M., J. Wilmore and S. Fox. *Health and Fitness Through Physical Activity.* New York: John Wiley and Sons, 1978.